FOREWARD

My name is Philip 'Sam' Davies. I w
Loughborough College, and now tl
annual turnover) child care compa
Football at Blackfield and Langley Football Club.

Since four years old I have always been fixated by football: all
levels through grass roots and up to the professional game. I have,
I believe, developed a significant understanding of the game at its
various levels.

I first encountered John Robson back in 2008/9. He was involved
at Alton Football Club at the time. However, I heard him speaking
at the Wessex League's AGM. What struck me was his clear, astute
understanding of the game and his effective use of humour to
underline the serious points he was making. This use of humour,
and his ability to connect with people, was undoubtedly one of his
greatest and most enduring skills.

At the start of the 2014/15 season, I approached John and offered
him the manager's job at Blackfield and Langley. We have developed
our close relationship since this point.

John is one of the most likeable people you could ever meet. His
knowledge of football is encyclopaedic alongside his determination
to remain abreast of current trends. This makes him a go-to man.

His analysis of player quality is also extremely strong; so if you want
opponents watched and accurately reported on ... he will do the
business.

In summary, John has devoted his life to football. He genuinely
loves the game. His knowledge and his enthusiasm are at times ...
unbelievable. More than this, he is a kind, supportive friend who it
is always a joy to spend time with.

4th September 2018

FAMILY

I was born on 3rd April 1947 in the mining village of Oakenshaw, County Durham, with a population of about a thousand. We lived at house No 4, Institute Street, which flooded when it rained. The Elliots were at No 1, the Grays at No 2 and the Peacocks at No 3. We most times didn't suffer, unless it poured, when it could reach No 6, the Mackies. There were sixteen houses in our street.

A zinc bath hung outside in our yard; there was no toilet as we know today, just a bench in a 'midden' which was two steps up, with a hole to sit on. There was access in the street, so that the midden men could come on Mondays and lift the access plate in the road and shovel the excrement into their wagon, before they threw powder into the areas, which had a much better odour than the stuff they threw into their wagon!

My dad, John, would sometimes come home as black as the ace of spades, but my mam had brought the bath in, stood it in front of the coal fire, while opening the drawer on the fire to the area where she could boil the water for dad's bath. It would take approximately half an hour before my mam, Bessie, could pot enough hot water, so my dad could clean himself up. My older sister Rosalind and I sat in the kitchen-cum-front room while dad had his bath, and got ready to have his meal. We all sat at the table for this.

Those days, most women were housewives, doing everything indoors. Cooking to prepare meals for their husbands was the priority, and it took me eight years to realise that Monday was fry-up day, which I loved, and still do, being the left-overs from Sunday's dinner. Wednesday was a homemade pie, and potatoes with gravy, and Friday was fish and chips, bought from the fish shop situated about thirty yards from the bottom of our street. This was a corrugated building painted green, where I used to help out on a Friday, keeping the supply of chips on hand, using the chip-making machine. My pocket money from that was sixpence for about one and a half hours and a bag of chips topped with cooked batter from the fish, which I loved.

When I was five years old, if my dad wasn't working, he would take me to watch the football, on the top field, where, if the numbers

Tony, I hope you enjoy my book, Robbo.

Family, Football and Friends

by John 'Robbo' Robson

SHORT BOOKS

First published 2019

by the Short Publishing Company Ltd
Winchester
Hampshire SO23 0JG
England

Set in Cambria 11pt
Designed and typeset by the Short Publishing Company Ltd
Cover designed by Victoria Kochowski
Printed in Great Britain by Menzies Response

CONTENTS

were available, the men would set up the goals (no nets). Someone who had brought a whistle would ref, and a couple of the lads would act as linesmen. On one of the Sunday matches, after church, the referee awarded a penalty. I let go of my dad's hand and ran behind the goal. The penalty was scored and the old leather ball hit me full on the chest, causing a collapsed lung. As I was knocked out, the ambulance from the mine was brought to take me to hospital, with a medic and my dad in the back. By all accounts, not realising how bad I was, I was put in an iron lung for a while until I recovered. The only good thing was that I missed school for a few weeks, but I missed football more!

When I was ten my mam and dad, Rosalind and I were offered a new council house in Willington, a town three miles down the road. Willington got to Wembley in the amateur cup final and were drawn against Bishop Auckland. According to the League then, Bishop were supplying the amateur internationals' team with three players, but Willington put three goals past them before half time, and went on to win 4-1, and the attendance was the biggest ever for an amateur cup final, and I think still is, as the new Wembley only holds 90,000. According to my Uncle Tommy, who was part of Willington FC, the celebrations were excellent. The goalkeeper, Jack Snowdon, is still living in Willington today.

Moving to Willington, into a new three-bedroomed house with running water, both hot and cold, was brilliant! On the other side of the road was a grassed area, perfect for football. It also allowed me to meet and make new friends, namely, Alan Franks (Franksie), George Fawcett (Geordie), Tony Rosethorne (Tone) and Robson, known as Robbo. Robson is a common name in the north east, and as we had all moved, more or less at the same time, I being another Robson, was nicknamed Rop, after my dad. Don't ask why!

We all lived in Canterbury Crescent, and formed a five-a-side team who challenged the other boys on our estate to a game. As the Hall Lane estate was to us massive, we could easily find teams ready to play us, win or lose, which was brilliant! After forming a hall lane team, we regularly played the bottom estate, known as the bottom-enders, and the top estate, divided by the railway lines. The good thing was we were always at home, given our area opposite, until they started to build Norwich Gardens on our pitch, which became smaller and smaller because of the need for new houses.

Because we had three bedrooms in 25 Canterbury Crescent, I think our mam and dad thought they could have another addition to our family, not worrying if it was a boy or girl as 'it' would fit in my room or my sister Rosalind's bedroom. As luck had it, I kept my bedroom for myself, and my lovely sister, Anne, was born. Now the Robson family was complete and generally happy. Within a couple of months, in September 1958, I was to join my new school. It was a brand new secondary modern school, with all of the facilities needed. It was a ten-minute walk from 25 Canterbury Crescent. Perfect! My new uniform, which every student wore, made me feel intelligent! But that didn't last long; I was average apart from sport, which I loved.

Football, athletics and tennis were my schooling, sitting by the window, looking out onto the playing field, although woodwork and art I enjoyed. Mr Marsden, our PE teacher, covered the exercise we needed, but was adamant that we had a good athletics team. Sprinting and hurdles were my favourites, as we never played football in PE classes.

When you are a lad and you have ambitions, whether in sport or academics, you dream of wanting to play at Wembley, or going to university and leaving with degrees. However, I knew it was the Wembley dream for me. All I wanted to do was to be successful playing football. Being a coal miner, my dad just wanted his children to enjoy life, and coming from a man who spent half of his life hundreds of feet below ground, my two sisters and myself listened intently to our parents. How lucky were we regarding our mam and dad! Yet I felt I needed to move away from home to fulfil my dream.

My dad once mentioned joining the Army and seeing the world, 'You will stay fit, play sport and see the world.'

This was in my mind every time I looked at the same buildings and the same people, doing the same things. With that constantly in my mind, I decided to visit an Army Careers recruiting office with one of my mates, and after listening to this young corporal, we decided to sign a form, which we thought was not a definite, as we were going to a junior boys' camp in Scotland, Troon to be exact, on the Ayrshire coast, to learn our trade. But after six months, I was told I was being posted to Germany, and looking back this was the beginning of my life as a man, and as a soldier, and also a footballer.

ARMY FOOTBALL

I enjoyed Troon and Scotland very much, but little did I know, I would be sold-on-loan to St Johnstone in Perth in a few years time.

On 10th October 1965 I was put on a plane and posted to Hamelin, the Pied Piper's town, Germany. I landed in Hannover airport and was picked up by Gilbert Boniface and driven to my new home in Hamelin, a bridging regiment with barrack room blocks. After checking into the guard room I picked up my needs, and walked to my block, found my room, and was introduced to my room mates. Jumbo Williams, Terry Neil and my driver, Gilbert Boniface, all black lads who, apart from playing dominoes until the early hours, became very good friends.

As yet, my mind was concentrating on being a good soldier, while also wanting to represent the regimental team, and hopefully the brigade, and maybe the BAOR XI. Being fortunate, I managed to achieve these aims, while also playing for a German team, Bad Pyrmont, on a Sunday, which I enjoyed immensely, while learning my German.

After having enjoyed my three years in Germany, I was posted to Nicosia, Cyprus to be a driver to Colonel Parker, the head of the United Nations and the peace-maker between Archbishop Makarios and General Grivas. There were two good parts to the job: we started work at 6 am and finished at 4.30 pm, which left the evenings to relax, before playing football for our regiment, 42 Squadron, in the League, as it was too hot in the afternoons.

It didn't take us long to make our way up the League, beating Dakelio Bravo who were top, at their place, and after a few more games we found ourselves top of the League unbeaten. Mind you, having players like Steve Johnstone, Stan Patrick and Joe Goodall, we ended up winning the League and Cup double.

When serving in the United Nations peace-keeping force in Cyprus, you only serve a six-month posting, and though the time passed quickly, I managed to write to my future wife, Ann, every day, and my family in Willington, County Durham every week. At Lloyds Bank in Greenwich, my girlfriend, Ann, was asked what I looked like, but all of the photos of me were in football strip. When I got home and met her work colleagues they said I wasn't recognisable in trousers and a shirt, and thought all I had done was play football for six months, especially as I had a tan! Back home and a few weeks leave in Plumstead in South East London, I asked Ann if she would come up north with me to meet my mam, dad and sisters, and I was really pleased when she said, 'Yes.' My only worry was that Willington, County Durham, was totally different from London, but the visit went well and she loved the warmth of the people. After a few days we went back to London. From there I was posted to 27 Regiment, which was stationed just outside Salisbury. On 3rd May 1969 Ann and I were married at Plumstead church. My family travelled down for the wedding and to this day it was the best day of my life. We were given married quarters in the camp, and after a few months were moved within the camp to a brand new flat. Darren, our son, was born between the moves and he loved it, forever throwing my medals and trophies out from the balcony of the flat.

After a couple of months, I was fortunate to be asked to go to Aldershot for the trials to play for the British Army XI. After training for three days of friendlies, I was selected to play in the No 9 shirt alongside Alfie Coulton, who was a regular in the Army XI. On my return to my regiment feeling very pleased with myself, Amesbury FC, who were approximately four miles down the road, asked me to join them. I asked the Army for permission and Major Foster, my boss, said, 'Yes', as long as I was insured. At my first game on the Saturday, unknown to me, a scout from Swindon Town was watching our left half, who was a good player, and as we had won the game, we were told of Swindon Town's interest. On the following Monday I was called into Major Foster's office to be told Swindon Town FC wanted me to go up for trials. Major Foster said, 'Yes', as long as I was insured. I went to the county ground and met Don Rogers, the Manager, who after he had spoken to the scout and seen me, asked me to turn out for their reserves on the following Saturday at Newbury. However, the paperwork was delayed and I was called up to play for the Army midweek, and had to forget Swindon Town. I also had to cancel my registration with Amesbury Town FC.

Given that the British Army team were used to, hopefully, attracting young men to join the Army, we played at some fantastic venues all around the country, and we were seen as close to being professionals. The Kentish Cup was played against the Belgian Army and the French Army, who had National Service. We played in front of big crowds away from home, in places like Anderlecht and Paris. We were playing against top professionals. At Anderlecht, in the away dressing room, there were plaques above the numbered pegs with the names of the Manchester United players who were on the plane when the Munich air disaster happened, since Man U had played Anderlecht in the previous round, both home and away. It was a lovely tribute to a great team.

While playing for the Army XI we competed in the Kentish Cup, a cup which has been played for since 1928. In the late 60s and early 70s France, Belgium and our Army XI competed for this cup. The good news for us was that when we went over the Channel we knew we would be playing in big stadiums and in front of big crowds. We played France, in Paris at PSG's ground and, although we lost, on the night, it proved to be a great experience. We also played at Anderlecht in front of a big crowd, some 28,000, and yet once again we lost.

Our problem was that all these countries still had National Service, which meant we were playing against top professionals and, in some games, internationals. In 1973, as a unit, we won the Army Cup 2-1 against the winners of the British Army of the Rhine Cup (28 (BR) Signal Regt) at the stadium on Queens Avenue in Aldershot. Our unit, the RCT Training Centre, also won the NAAFI Jubilee Cup in 1973, where I managed to score a goal, beating the RAF and Navy champions. That season my team, Sunderland, who I supported, and still do, beat Leeds Utd 1-0. Leeds were one of the top teams at the time. Ian Porterfield's goal proved to be a great win, after a few fantastic saves from Jim Montgomery our goalie. Stevie Johnson and I went to Wembley. Stevie, another Black Cats supporter serving in the Navy, was a good mate, and today is working for the FA.

Army vs Coventry City

While I was playing for the British Army XI in 1974 we were told that Coventry City FC were coming to Aldershot stadium to take part in a game against the Army XI in respect for their General Manager, the Army team captain, the legend that is Joe Mercer. Now usually in games like this, teams of the stature of Coventry City field mostly reserves, but to their credit we were playing against their first XI of: Bill Glazier (GK), Paul Cahill (2), Micky Coop (3), J. Craven (4), (Captain), A. Dugdale (5), W. Smith (6), M. Maguire (7), L. Cartwright (8), A. Green (9), M. Ferguson (10) and A. Robinson (11); and on their bench: J. Blyth (12), D. Nardiello (13), B. Roberts (14) and T. O'Brien (15). Joe Mercer was their General Manager, with Gordon Milne, Team Manager and T Casey their Trainer. What a great experience for our squad! To cap it all, the newly installed floodlights in the stadium at Queen's Avenue were to be switched on for its first game. Perfect! But this was going to be a test for the Army XI.

I started the game up top in the No 10 shirt with Alfie Coulton alongside me. At that time our Coach was Bill Stoves, who we all respected for his knowledge of the game, so whatever he asked of us we tried to carry out, and if it wasn't working then on our bench we had: J Slade (12), P Brown (13), Davey Steadman (14), the late Tony Cox (15), Micky Doig (17) and J Dudley (16). Bill would not hesitate to change things if we were on the back foot. Mike Varney was our physio, who, when he left the Army joined Tottenham Hotspur and carried on his great career with them.

Bill Stoves was a big believer in his players socialising and his wife Kathy looked after us when we got together at their place. Back to the game, yes, they beat us, but we gave them a good game, even though we lost. After the match we were given a chance to get to know the Coventry City players, which gave us an insight into professional football at the highest level. They were travelling back in their coach the following morning.

When I returned to my job as a soldier, my Commanding Officer called me into his office to explain that Mr Mercer had asked if I was allowed to travel back to Coventry with their players and spend time with the first team, training. The CO asked how I would feel about the offer. 'Yes, please,' I said, then went home to my family quarters to explain to my wife what was happening. With that I packed a small case and drove back to the barracks to board their coach. When I boarded it I was met with boos from every player, but as they died down Mr Mercer asked me my nickname. 'Robbo,' I said and sat down looking forward to the journey. A few skits came from the players, especially when I told them Sunderland was the team I supported. Once again came the boos, so I came back with, 'Well, we beat Leeds Utd 1-0 in the FA Cup final last season, and yes I went to Wembley.' Anyway the players settled down as we got on our way. I couldn't stop wondering why I had been asked to make the journey.

As we arrived in the car park at Coventry City, the players said 'Cheerio' and Gordon Milne told the players '10 am at the training ground in the morning, for a 10.30 start.' He then turned to me, saying, 'I will be with you in a minute.' As the staff emptied the training gear from the coach I lent a hand. Gordon then came to me and said, 'Put your gear in my boot and I will take you to your digs.' After no more than 15 minutes we pulled into the training ground, where they had an apartment for me. I soon settled in, unpacked, but realised I hadn't brought a clock. Anyway, I had a phone on the bedside cabinet. I tried the phone, but for some unknown reason, it was only geared for incoming calls. Anyway, before I got settled, one of the lads came in and asked if all was OK. 'Yes,' I said. 'Well, put a jacket on, we are going for a Chinese in town.' The next thing, we were heading into town, with two of the lads in the back of the car, the driver and myself. It wasn't long before we parked and were walking to the Chinese.

Quite a few people on the short walk were saying their hellos to the players and to be fair, they were stopping and chatting to the supporters. On entering the Chinese, the boys were once again answering everyone. The players went upstairs; the stairs went up through the middle of the restaurant, so up we went, turning at the top to find a waiter showing us to our tables. We made the orders, both food and drinks, and sat chatting, although I was doing more listening, as the waiter took the order to the kitchens. Before the food and drink had been served, I needed the toilet. After no more than ten minutes, I came back to my table, only to find the boys had vanished and the manager was standing there, very serious, telling me I owed them £240. As the food was cooking and the drinks were on the way, I looked at him and tried to explain, but he was adamant, I had to pay the bill. I had about thirty pounds on me and there were no cards in the 1970s.

'You must leave,' the manager said. 'I will be reporting this to the club. What is your name?' 'John Robson', I said. 'You must leave now.' I slowly walked down the stairs,' with those in the Chinese watching me. I felt terrible as I closed the door into the street. I was lost, but only for about 30 seconds, when out the players came from every shop doorway, clapping their hands, then we walked back into the restaurant up the stairs to our tables. You never forget a prank like that, with people who everyone knows. Phew, was I relieved! Mind you, I didn't enjoy my food as I normally would. The manager was laughing, along with the other customers.

My few days with the boys were great, but after those few days I was called back to Aldershot, to play in the Army Cup preliminary round, as we were the holders of the Army Cup, having won it in 1973. As it happened, I didn't return to Coventry, due to football and family. However, I contacted Coventry to say thank you.

Northern Ireland

On my return from Cyprus, after my six months with the United Nations Force in Nicosia in 1969, I was serving at the RCT (Royal Corps of Transport) Depot Barracks in Aldershot. The RCT was formerly known as the RASC (Royal Army Service Corps). I was in charge of the three-ton Army trucks. One Thursday afternoon, the 16th July, my Commanding Officer called me into his office; I thought to chat about football, however I was wrong. I went in quite relaxed, but soon found myself thinking, 'Oh yes, I'm a soldier first and a footballer second!' On Sunday 19th July, because of the trouble in Northern Ireland, 3 Paratroop Brigade had been told they were going to be the first troops to go in and were flying out to Belfast. I sat there thinking why is the boss, Major Pip Coan, telling me this in his office? As I had never jumped out of an aeroplane in my life! Then came the explanation. One of the Paratroopers lived in, and came from Belfast, and because of the risk to himself as a soldier, he couldn't go. Major Coan then said that I had to go in his place, and could I turn up at 3 Paratroop Brigade for riot squad drill that afternoon, ready to fly out to Northern Ireland on Sunday. I didn't ask any questions, I just turned up to 3 Para Barracks and reported to their guard room at 1.30 pm. Just to fill you in, my beret was black, but if you were a paratrooper, you usually turned up at a new destination by jumping out of a plane from 20,000 feet, wearing their red beret. Anyone not wearing a red beret was called a 'crap' hat, so for the next six months I was to be known as the 'crap' hat. After a couple of days training to be part of the riot squad, I was then told to be ready to fly out to Northern Ireland on Sunday morning. When I went home on the Thursday evening and told Ann, she didn't believe me, but at least she did on Monday while listening to the news on TV.

We were housed in a school assembly hall off the Newtownards Road in Belfast. Also, we were briefed into being ready and kitted out for duty. I was terrified while waiting for the call, even though these guys had done this all over the world, and I could see they looked forward to it. We had landed and made our way to our quarters when Captain Maynard got the call. There was a crowd, estimated at 1,500 to 2,000, congregating in the Newtownards Road, looking to make their way to a club at the bottom of that road. We had to be on the trucks within five minutes to take an alternative route to the bottom of the road, to be ready as a riot squad. I feel there is no reason to explain what happened, just to say there was no trouble that evening and we dispersed after some 45 minutes. Success after the first riot squad assembly! It was just another job to 3 Para; to me it wasn't just another job. Was it going to be like this for six months, sleeping on a wooden floor, while being on alert 24 hours a day? Thank goodness it wasn't! After five or six weeks, things started calming down. Friday, Saturday and Sunday evenings were riot squad alert, but from Monday to Friday we kept fit for duty, but were allowed to kick a ball on the school field. We were also allowed to mingle with the locals in our immediate area.

One day, I wandered down the Newtownards Road, having been given permission from our Captain. I stopped after hearing some young boys playing football in a cul-de-sac, so I wandered in to watch, leaning on a lamppost. After they kicked a few loose passes, an elderly gentleman approached me, and, as I was in uniform, asked me if I was allowed to come to his house and meet his wife and have tea with them. I told him I would have to get permission from our CO who said, 'Yes, as long as it's on a week day.' The following day I went back to the cul-de-sac at about 6 pm and the boys were out there with the ball.

After less than five minutes, the elderly gentleman asked me if I was able to come to his place for tea. 'Yes, I was given permission.' With that, we exchanged names, and shook hands. 'I'm John,' I said, 'John Robson.' 'George,' he replied, so we watched the boys, exchanging ideas about why I was in Belfast. He said he was pleased we were there as the trouble had died down, apart from Fridays and Saturdays. While exchanging our thoughts, we arrived, after some 30 yards, at the front door of George's terraced house. In we went and I was introduced to his wife, Elsie. As we sat down to our tea, cakes and sandwiches, I noticed some photos on the top of their old free-standing piano. Pictures of George Best. After finishing my sandwich and taking a drink of my tea, I asked, 'Are you a fan of George?'

'He is our grandson,' Elsie replied, saying, 'He was called after his grandad.' George nodded, as I said, 'You both must be very proud.' Which I knew they were, after listening to George. 'You must have been a good player, George.' 'I was OK, John,' he said while Elsie pulled a face and looked at me, saying, 'Yes.' While I was in Belfast I visited them four or five times, not always for tea. When I returned home after my six months they wrote to me. While serving in Belfast I received invites from Gibby McKenzie (Portadown FC) and 'the' Denis Viollet (Linfield). Both managers of their clubs wanted me to sign. They were asked to apply to the British Army Sports Control Board. It appeared in the local paper in Northern Ireland, but once again nothing came of it.

I was back in Aldershot in January 1970, after an experience I probably needed as a solider. 3 Para were soldiers. Not long after, I was picked to play in a trial for the British Army squad. Luckily, I was asked to join the squad and started in a game against the Royal Navy at the Pitt Street ground in Portsmouth. Thanks to Alfie Coulton and Dougie Aitchinson, I had a good game and we beat them 2-0. I got two goals, while Eddie Green in goal and Joe Ramsden, Steve Morton, Alan Goucher and Bruce Menzies, our back four, kept a clean sheet. We went on to beat the RAF at Aldershot, winning the Inter-Services Cup. I was chosen for the Combined Services team, meeting up with some of the players who I played against in the Inter-Services Cup, namely Geordie Welsh, scouse 'Johno' Johnston and Kenny Oram. Our get-together was a trip to Gibraltar to play their international side at the stadium near the airport, combined with a few days tour of the rock, apes, internal reservoirs and the stalagmites and stalactites cathedral.

MY FOOTBALL CAREER

Back from Northern Ireland in 1970, Ann and I and Darren were together again, but in an awful married quarter on the outskirts of Bulford Camp. Not a good house to bring up a family. It was February, with no heating! Within a few weeks, we were moved to a new apartment on the other wide of the barracks, with heating and all the comforts to bring up a family.

Within two weeks of settling, and shortly after being selected for the Army XI, I was asked to play for Amesbury FC. Their ground was just five miles down the road, so I gained permission from Major Foster my CO, signed the insurance cover, and turned up at Amesbury at 1.30 p. for the 3 o'clock kick-off. I was introduced to the Chairman, Manager and players, then changed and out for the pre-match warm-up.

The one thing, which no one mentioned, was that a scout for Swindon Town was going to be at the match, to watch Amesbury's No 9. The game commenced and at half time, I had scored two goals and was looking forward to another 45 minutes, and when I managed to score three more. At the end of the game the scout asked permission to talk to me, No10. He took my name and said he would be recommending me to come to Swindon. I told him I was in the Army, stationed at Bulford Camp. 'No problem,' he said, things would be done properly. Within a couple of days Major Foster received an approach for me to go to the county ground for trials. The problem was that I was told to attend the Army XI at Aldershot and the dates coincided. When I explained my problem, obviously the Army XI took priority, which disappointed me. I made a call to Swindon Town, and they understood, saying they would give me another date for my trial, but it never happened. Joe Wilson, Manager of Brighton Hove Albion, had sent an approach but this was yet another possibility which didn't happen.

So there I was, playing on Wednesdays for the Army XI, when I received an invitation to play for Andover Town in the Southern League. The Walled Meadow was their ground, Jack Norris was their Chairman, and he and his lovely wife, Vera, became very good friends to me, Ann and our children, Darren and my new-born daughter Lisa. Travelling wasn't a problem, as I stayed at Jack and Vera's on a Friday evening, while Ann moved to her parents for the weekends. I remember one of our games was against Ashford Town, which as I was staying at my in-laws, was not too far up the road, in Middlesex. I remember getting there with time to spare, but couldn't find the ground. I started to ask a few blokes where the football ground was, only to find there was no football ground, only a rugby ground. I then decided to find the police station, and the PC I spoke to said, 'I think you will find Ashford Town is in Kent.' He then said, if I could get hold of someone in Kent, I could explain things. 'Thank you,' I said. After speaking to Jack, our Chairman, who, while being disappointed understood my predicament, then set off for Ashford, arriving just as the game ended 2-2. Jack was OK with me and the players and staff thought, 'typical, a thick Northerner!' which I accepted.

While still playing with Andover, I received approaches asking me to join other clubs in the area around Portsmouth and Southampton, one being Waterlooville FC, who were top of the Southern League, and Basingstoke FC, another big club. The Army had given me permission to take my Coaching badges; I knew they would be good for me, either as a Coach or Manager, when I couldn't play any more, but all I wanted to do was play, feeling coaching was years away.

Basingstoke also offered me a house and job if I signed for them, so after talking to Ann and both clubs, I accepted Basingstoke with Cliff Huxford the Manager, knowing I was due to come out of the Army soon. Prior to signing I had explained to Jack Norris, the Andover Manager and Waterlooville Chairman, Peter Faulkner, and I signed for Basingstoke. After about seven or eight games, we were due to play Waterlooville at the Camrose Ground. I knew it was going to be a tough game, but luckily Tony Foster and me up front managed to score the goals to win 3-0.

Within 24 hours came another offer from Waterlooville, a private offer. I went to Peter Faulkner's house and met up with the Directors, and became a Waterlooville player. With Jim Storrie as my Manager and Peter my new Chairman, I felt I was settled in Waterlooville and my family likewise, and here in 2017, after three house moves within the area, we have settled and enjoyed our stay. 'Family, Football and Friends.' Just thinking about the 71-72 season, in one of my early games I was given a very good write-up in the programme by Gordon Carpenter of the Kent Messenger regarding our game against Maidstone United FC. Once again I got on the score sheet with a couple of goals, only to shake hands with the guy who marked me during the 90 minutes, none other than the England Manager, Roy Hodgson. I've kept the programme, hoping I could meet him and ask him to sign it. We came away winners that day, but obviously it didn't click with me that it was Roy Hodgson until much later, when he became Manager of England. I thoroughly enjoyed my stay at Waterlooville, and my chance to play for St Johnstone in the Scottish Division one, against the likes of Rangers, Hibs and Hearts in front of big crowds, both at home at Muirton Park and away. My only disappointment was that I didn't play against Celtic at Parkhead through injury.

Having left the Army, I was adapting to civilian life with my family, living in a Waterlooville club house and looking forward to honouring my contract, while attending college studying plumbing and heating, City and Guilds, at Eastleigh College, thanks to our Chairman Peter Faulkner. I felt that since I enjoyed learning my new trade and as I loved my football, I would be able to learn a trade and keep my family happy, but during college my wife Ann took a job at the Matchbox factory in the evenings, which helped us financially. Things seemed fine and the football was going well at Waterlooville. The club had very good support at the Jubilee Road stadium. My son Darren was attending school, while my daughter Lisa was four years old and our youngest, Scott, was just finding his feet. Things were going well, both on and off the field, the only problem being that Ann was an only child, with her mam and dad living in south-east London, while my family lived in the north east, so visiting their grandchildren wasn't easy. Although the club house was fine, we decided to look for a house in the area, which was easier for the schools, and ended up in 21 Silvester Road. Within a couple of visits to us, Alice and Jim, Ann's mam and dad, decided to move down near to us and found a lovely bungalow, no more than a quarter of a mile from us. They settled in well and really helped with the children. Regarding my family up north, we did our best to keep in touch by phone and letter, plus a couple of journeys home each year.

Immediately after leaving the Army

At the start of the 1974-75 season I had been given permission to sign for Winchester City FC, who at the time were playing their games at Airlie Road. Our fierce neighbours in those days were Basingstoke FC some twelve miles up the road. On this particular Tuesday night's game we murdered them 5-1 and I was fortunate to get on the score sheet three times. Little did I know that the Bristol City manager, Alan Dicks, had come to watch me. After the game our manager, my good friend Jack Norris, called me over and introduced me to Mr Dicks, who asked me if I would sign for his club. However, I explained that I was still in the Army. 'No problem,' he said, 'tomorrow I will phone the Army Control, and see about buying you out.' Jack Norris told me that Mr Dicks had offered Winchester City £10,000 for me. Within two days Bristol City were told they could not buy me out. Major Dobson refused to let me out, even though I was due out of the Army within eighteen months, yet a couple of years on, Guy Whittingham bought himself out for £250 to play at Portsmouth. I still don't understand it to this day. After several approaches from Joe Wilson of Brighton FC, I was still Corporal John Robson and still in the Army.

During the remainder of my Army service Basingstoke asked me to sign for them. Cliff Huxford was an ex-Southampton FC player and a friend through football, and they had been promoted, but I was enjoying my football with Winchester City under my other manager and friend, Jack Norris. Jack and Vera, his wife, would let me stay at their home in Highfield Road in Andover for away games, but Jack said, 'John, it's another step up the ladder, join Basingstoke.' I joined Cliff and the players at Basingstoke and played alongside Tony Foster, a natural goal scorer, and we got on like a partnership made in heaven. I was the target and Tony played off me. We settled in, in no time, enjoying a good run in the League and cups.

Then one Saturday we were drawn to play Waterlooville FC at the Camrose. On the day we played them off the park, winning 3-0 and lucky for me, I got a hat-trick. After a week or so, Cliff pulled me into his office to tell me that Waterlooville wanted me. Because I was still a soldier, no money changed hands. Out of respect, I said I would talk to Mr Peter Faulkner and his Directors at his home in Billett Avenue, a private road in Waterlooville. I realised when I arrived at Mr Faulkner's home, that the Rolls Royce, swimming pool, gym, games room etc. and his Directors sitting around his table, approximately eight in number, plus Peter, looked 'big time.' The offer they made me, as I was due to come out of the Army, could not be turned down. It was to sign a three-year contract, with a four-figure signing-on fee, and to go to Eastleigh College to train as a plumber and heating engineer, with bonuses written into my football contract. I signed on the dotted line.

I said to Peter and his Directors that if I wasn't living up to their expectations by 1st November, I would pay my signing on fee back. On the first of November I had scored over 20 goals, so everyone was happy. The club I had joined at Jubilee Road in Waterlooville, was managed professionally by the late Jim Storrie and Peter Faulkner and his Directors. Little did I realise this area would be my home for the next 40 plus years.

My footballing life at Waterlooville was ideal. Peter gave us a club house, 51 Jubilee Road, with a weekly rental of £8. My wife Ann would take the money to Peter's offices, some 50 yards from our house, and pay Terry Manns, the Club Secretary, the £8, but more often than not, Terry would say, 'It's OK this week, we won and John scored for us.' Peter had told him not to worry about the rent.

The Jubilee Road ground was owned by Peter Faulkner and was kept up to scratch week in and week out, which, with our success and good facilities, meant good support from around the area. For most games the big stand was full and all around the ground were our regular supporters, plus the opposition's supporters. When we had a good run in the FA Cup games and Hampshire Senior Cup, which we won a couple of times during the time I was there, and even on away games the regulars were there voicing their support. Under

Jim Storrie, who had played at Leeds Utd, as long as we worked hard when we lost the ball, but expressed our talent when we had the ball, he was happy.

Frankie Middleton took no prisoners on training nights, which meant we were fit and ready for every game. When Jim left the club, to go back to Scotland to manage Perth club, St. Johnstone, David Monks, ex-Sheffield United player, took over as Manager. David was a quiet man, unlike Jim Storrie, but soon got to know the boys, having moved down to Hampshire to continue his football career. However, after a mid-week game at home to Salisbury FC, Ian St John, the Portsmouth Manager, was up watching the game, which we won 3-0, of which I managed to score two. After the game, Peter, the Chairman, asked me to meet him so after my shower I made for the boardroom. In the room were a couple of Directors and a couple of Salisbury Directors, and Ian St John, who everyone knew from his Liverpool and Scotland days as a player. I sat down and was given a soft drink, waiting for our Chairman to come in. During the next 15 minutes Ian St John did not acknowledge me once but stayed talking to the Directors in one-word answers, which I thought was ill-mannered, and came across as, well, I'm better than you lot. Peter arrived and apologised to Ian St John, to which he got no reply. I then sat down with Peter and St John, while the others in the room left, knowing a business discussion was about to take place. Peter introduced me to St John, saying that he had been watching me, with the possibility of signing me at Portsmouth. Still St John had not said one word to me. 'What do you think, John?' Ian St John said nothing, so I stood up, said my thank you, apologising to Peter, and left the boardroom to go for a drink with our players and the Salisbury boys.

The following day Peter Faulkner asked me to meet him in his office. His words were, 'I'm glad you are still with us, John, but why?' I explained why to Peter, which he accepted. He then told me that Jim Storrie, our old Manager, wanted me at St Johnstone on the Saturday, for the first League game of the Scottish season versus Glasgow Rangers. If I would go they would fly me up to Glasgow early Saturday and taxi me to Ibrox for the game. I spoke to Ann, my wife, and she left any decision up to me. Knowing Jim Storrie and a chance to go back to Scotland, where I had enjoyed my 18 months at Dundonald Camp, Troon, I said, 'Yes.' On Saturday morning Ron

Stanton picked me up from home and took me to Gatwick Airport to catch the plane to Scotland.

St Johnstone FC

Both John Greig and Tam Forsythe sat with me during our after-game meal, and told me I would do well in Scotland. Both were centre halves for Rangers and Scotland, and John Greig was Captain of the club and country. I felt that for the 85 minutes I was on the pitch, they thought I had done well, even though Rangers beat us. My 1976-77 season had started well, given I had left home with our Vice Chairman, Ron Stanton, at 4 am for Gatwick; our flight to Glasgow had left at 7.15 am; then a taxi to the Argyle Hotel to meet my new team mates, and club officials. On arrival, Jim Storrie the Manager, was in reception with the Chairman waiting for us. I wasn't even thinking I would be starting the game, then after I had met all the players and staff, including our physio Jim Peacock, who was also the Scottish Physio, Jim said, 'I want you to start up top, but don't worry about set pieces, just be a nuisance.' When walking out on to the Ibrox pitch to a full house, I felt the pressure, while also feeling how lucky I was to be starting the 76-77 season here at Ibrox. Eighty-five minutes after the referee started the game, I came off to cheers of applause, or was that for Gordon McGregor who was taking my place for the last five minutes? On the way back to Perth, I asked Jim Storrie where I was staying. It was in the Salutation Hotel in Perth city centre. The coach dropped me off, I checked in to my room, phoned Ann, then lay on my bed, pondering and tired, very tired, remembering I must phone Ron Stanton to say thank you, and ask what he thought of the game, and how his journey home was.

Sunday morning 10.30 am and I had missed breakfast. I had a shower, went down to reception and asked for directions to Muirton Park. I then stepped out of the hotel and thought, 'I need to know where we are training at 10.30 on Monday.' As I made my way to Muirton, St Johnstone's ground, quite a few people said their hellos, which reminded me of home, where people who don't know you, yet saying their hellos or good mornings, which made me feel good.

Arriving at the ground, I looked for the players' entrance, which, to my surprise was open. I walked along the corridor, hearing male voices, and arrived at the treatment room. I knocked and Jim

23

Peacock opened the door, inviting me in asking, 'Is anything wrong?' 'No,' I said. 'I felt I needed to know where we were training in the morning.'

Jim was treating Duncan Lambie, our flying winger, who had obviously taken a knock in the match. Jim offered me a lift back to the hotel, but I thanked him, saying I was OK, I wanted to walk back to get to know the area. Lunch at the hotel was 12.30 until 2 pm so, although I was hungry, having not had breakfast, I felt walking back would kill a bit of time before lunch.

Back at the hotel, I was introduced to Mrs Brown, the hotel Manager, who, after a chat, told me the table for one was in the corner of the dining room with my name on it and that would be my table for all meals. With that she showed me to the dining room and then to my table, saying, 'You are going to be here for a while.' I couldn't complain about my room, as it was in the staff quarters, on the top floor of the hotel, and once I got to know the workers they would keep me in touch with what was going on, as the basement was a very large theatre area with a stage, bar and seating for the entertainers appearing at the hotel. Billy Connolly appeared there, and many more who were making their way in the entertainment business. I felt I was being well looked after by St Johnstone so felt that I must give my best to the club.

On the Monday morning, Jim had told us to be at Muirton for a discussion regarding our Saturday game at Ibrox to go through the system we played and where we needed to put things right on the pitch. Dress code: training gear. As I wasn't in possession of any training gear, I thought it would be right to be early. Some of the players and staff had to travel to the club from all over, as I found out later. I set off at 9.30 am, walking to Muirton Park, allowing myself 30 minutes to get there, as we had to be ready to start by 10.30 am. Knowing Jim from my days at Waterlooville you didn't turn up late, you were always ready to start at the time given.

I got to the club ground just after 10 am and Jim and the staff were there, setting out a circuit on the pitch, so I said to Jim, 'Have I any training kit, boss?' 'It's on your peg in the home dressing room.' 'Thanks, boss,' was my reply and into the home dressing room I went, to find my kit on the No 9 peg and our Captain, Phil Roberts, an Englishman, signed from Grimsby in 1974. Within about ten minutes the whole of the squad who had been involved at Ibrox in our first League game were ready for training. Jim Peacock, the physio, came in and with clipboard and pen in his hand went to every player, asking if we had any aches, knocks, or breathing problems after the Rangers game. Apart from Duncan Lambie, who had received treatment on the Sunday after the game, everyone seemed OK, then Jim Storrie asked me how I felt after the 90 minutes. My answer was typical of that of a player, 'Knackered, boss.' 'Well, that's not surprising considering you were up at 4 am, then flew up to Glasgow and played 85 minutes against one of the top sides in Europe.' 'Thanks, boss,' was my reply, but I knew I still had a lot to learn at this level.

The next game was against Montrose on Tuesday at home in the League Cup, but I knew we had work to do regarding set pieces and a system to suit the new signings which Jim had made prior to the season, starting against Rangers. When we were all there, Jim spoke to us regarding the things we needed to work on. The talk lasted about an hour, then it was all changed and out on the pitch to go through the important bits that should make us more productive when we had possession and less vulnerable when we defended. We worked for about an hour on shape and the system Jim needed us to play at home and away, which reminded me of the Waterlooville system we played at home. This helped me enormously, mind you: the system he wanted to play away from home was much more defensive-minded and even at centre forward I had to do my jobs when we didn't have the ball. The good news was, we beat Montrose in the League Cup game 1-0 and while it worked, on Saturday we were at home to Hibernian, a much bigger challenge to prepare for.

After another couple of days' training, even though it was light preparation for Saturday's game, I felt much more at home, both with the club staff and players; so much so that we played well to earn a draw at home and beat them away in the League Cup. In the League, we had Hamilton 'Accies' in the League away. Their No 9 was a player called Ted McDougall, soon to travel south to England to First Division clubs who were keen to sign him.

While my football was going well, my life away from the games and training was mostly spending time in my hotel room and phoning Ann, speaking to the children, and getting the odd call from mates asking, 'How is it going Robbo?'

Don't get me wrong: players would have given their right arm to be in my position, staying in a posh hotel, playing football at a high level, getting very well paid and making friends, but 50% of football and 50% of sitting in a hotel room watching TV was beginning to take its toll. People who know me, know I am not a drinker and while there was a drinking culture in football in the 1970s, I never noticed it with St. Johnstone, as the squad came from far and wide across Perth, and games or training, the boys were on their way home after either. Jim Peacock used to drop me back to my hotel in the city centre, then drive home.

While football meant almost everything to me, Ann and my children were living life without their husband and dad. This, and my evenings, living 700 miles away from them, made me ask my Chairman, Jim McKinley, if we could meet for a chat. 'No problem at all, John,' was the answer. Our Chairman was a very busy man, both in business and in football, yet he came to the hotel one Monday morning while I explained how I was feeling after my six weeks at St Johnstone, he listened, then asked me if we could get Ann to come up to Perth. I phoned Ann that evening, asking her to come up to Perth on the Chairman's request and flown up by the club. Within a couple of days Ann had arranged for her mother to look after the children for a few days, allowing her to travel up. Ann arrived, and first of all, it was great to see her. We sat in the hotel chatting about the children, and my new life in Perth, as a professional footballer. Ann realised how much my football meant to me, but at the same time was keenly aware of the distance between us.

As we were discussing things over a cup of tea, Jim McKinley walked in and shook Ann's hand, then sat down with us, asking for a cup of tea. We sat and chatted about the football and my concerns when not playing; being back in my hotel and 700 miles from my family. Jim McKinley then said to us, 'My car is outside. Would you mind coming with me, as I have something to show you?' With that we went outside and got into the car.

'Perth is a beautiful area,' he said, as we set off, 'I want to show you the North Inch. It's not far from the city centre and has remarkable views in every direction.'

Twenty minutes later we pulled up on the North Inch and got out of the car, admiring the stunning views across the water. With that, he said, 'Follow me, I've got something to show you both,' and we arrived at a bungalow, which hadn't long been built. Jim McKinley walked to the front door, took out some keys, and inside the three of us went. Four bedrooms, a large lounge, fitted kitchen and dining room, double garage, with a front garden and the stunning views mentioned. The Chairman then turned to us both and said, 'I will give you both time to think, but this bungalow will be yours, if you are willing to sign a three-year contract with us. The club will pay for the move, including furniture etc., and your contract will be reviewed every year the bungalow will be yours.'

He knew we wouldn't make a decision there and then, saying, 'Take your time, both of you, and John you can let me know when you are ready.'

Ann and I looked at each other, realising what a very good offer this was, but also knowing there were family matters which needed to be sorted. We got back into Jim McKinley's car and drove back to the hotel. As we said our thanks and cheerios, and as the Chairman drove off, we looked at each other, trying to take in what had been offered to us and our family.

The next day, Ann returned to London, then down to Waterlooville, while I spoke to Peter Faulkner, my Chairman, at Waterlooville, asking what he thought. There were so many opinions, both for and against, from those I asked. I wanted to speak to my mother and father, for their views, but they didn't have a phone, and writing back and forth would have taken ages.

When Ann got home and the kids were in bed, we talked over the pros and cons of the move. Financially, we would be much better off, but would the move be right for my family? Most of the advice I was given was that it was too good an offer to turn down. I was already on an excellent wage, with bonuses. My dad was earning £45 pounds per week as a coal miner, for six days underground, in darkness, with a day off on Sundays, while I was earning more than 20 times that, plus extras and the only time I was in darkness at work was when the floodlights failed. I don't think I gave too much thought to my children, i.e. their friends and schooling, or having visits in Scotland from family, but Ann soon put me right when she said how happy they were. This made me think just how much adjustment they would have to make, leaving all they loved about friends, relations and the area where we lived on the coast in Hampshire. Ann had also been moved from pillar to post when I was in the Army, but this move was far greater. This wasn't like moving from Aldershot to Basingstoke or Waterlooville, this was very much a life-changing move for all five in my family.

Jim Storrie, Jim Peacock and the players were aware of the offer regarding the house, if I signed a three-year contract, while the only people who mattered were myself, my wife and children. I also realised that the club needed an answer over the next five days.

As I said earlier, I loved playing football and at this level, being the highest I had played, the decision was, or could be, life-changing for me and my family. However, at present I had a choice to make. I did ask Jim Storrie and Jim McKinley to allow me until the end of the week. Then after the game at Hibernian I would give them my decision.

'No problem,' they said. We played Hibs and it was a great game with a full house. I managed to score and I'm sure they felt I would sign when we got together in the hotel on the Sunday morning. I didn't sleep much that night, yet after I realised how much it meant for my family to be asked to move again, I had made my decision. When they turned up at the hotel and we sat down for a chat I made my thank yous to Jim and the Chairman for everything both of them and the players had done during my short stay in Perth, but I owed it to my family to go back to Hampshire, knowing that either injury or loss of form would leave me in an area where I wasn't known, which would make it difficult regarding work outside of football. They both understood, yet still tried to offer reasons for me to stay. But my mind was made up, and I wanted to be fair to Peter Faulkner, Chairman at Waterlooville, who had helped me when I came out of the Army, regarding housing and sending me to college to become qualified in a trade outside of football.

After lunch I rang Ann and told her, then I rang Peter to explain my decision. Both parties seemed pleased, but would I be pleased in a couple of months? There was a clause in my contract to say that however long I was at St Johnstone, if and when I left, I was to go back to Waterlooville, and that is what I did. Goodbye and thank you for everything, St Johnstone FC.

To this day I can only tell you that, as I chose to come back to Hampshire, I have been fortunate to have had a good life being involved in football. I have three children, who have good jobs and have given Ann and me seven grandchildren. Darren, our oldest, was a very good footballer, playing at Conference level and also playing for me at Worthing, while I was their Manager, and he is now a civil servant, married to Sue and happy living in Portsmouth. He gave us three grandchildren, Henry, Adam and Rose with his first wife, Kerry. My daughter Lisa, who is married to Pete, has given us two grandsons, namely Joseph, 13 years old and Oliver who is eleven. Their mum was a very good athlete, competing as a sprinter and hurdler at county level.

Scott, my youngest, was also a good footballer, playing up top in the No 9 shirt, and scoring for his teams as a boy, but failed to carry it on when he was 16. He now works for the BBC licensing body. Golf is his pastime nowadays. He and Lisa, his wife, have given us two lovely granddaughters, Ella who is now 16 and training to be a hairdresser, and Ava Joyce who is six and wants to be a gymnast, judging by the way she jumps about all the time!

Back to Hampshire
All of the way back on the Wednesday, I questioned myself as to whether I had done the right thing, and if I would regret it in later life? Since leaving home to join the Army, I had been moving, as you do, being in one place for a few months, then somewhere else at a minute's notice, so I should be used to it. But in the Army you are not in charge of where you go, you do it because it is orders. Mind you, you get plenty of sport and regarding football, the Army made sure I was available for the British Army squad wherever we were and whatever we were doing, apart from when on active service.

Peter Faulkner and David Munks, the new Manager, welcomed me back, as did the players at training. However, I didn't expect to start in Saturday's game against Aylesbury United, away, as the club had started really well under Dave Munks. Yes, I was sub, and managed the last 20 minutes. On the way back the lads were asking me why I was back at the 'Ville', so I joked and said I had missed them all, but now I was back.

Waterlooville FC (Home) and Farnborough FC

Having passed my City and Guilds in plumbing at Eastleigh College, I knew I would need a job, and felt capable of working as a plumber's mate. Ron Stanton, one of Waterlooville FC's Directors, had his own roofing business, mostly fitting flat roofs with bitumen and felt. So I thought, 'Yes, I will give it a go.'

He paired me with Micky Seymour, who also played for Waterlooville, after being released from Southampton FC. He was a good guy who was an excellent midfield player, and who became a very good friend. Between us, every Monday morning, we would discuss our previous game on Saturday, while loading our van and driving to the job. I was the 'gofer', while Mick was the roofer. We stood by the bitumen while it was being made pliable in the barrel with the gas burner. As soon as it was ready, I would lift and pour it for Mick to roll out the felt. Depending on the layers of felt, Mick would overlap the joints, making it all waterproof. When finished, we would load up and drive off to our next job, still talking football. I worked with Micky for approximately nine months, which I enjoyed very much, mostly because of our love for football.

The staff and players at Waterlooville were the envy of the clubs in Hampshire, due mainly to their professionalism. Jubilee Road, our ground, was always kept up to scratch, whether it was the pitch, or the buildings which made it a stadium, even the car park. Which non-League club had houses for players' families to move into, while they were looking for houses local to the areas around Waterlooville? This was due to the Chairman and the Directors all playing their part in making the club as professional as possible, giving our players and, more important, our supporters, the facilities needed to make their time at Jubilee Road as enjoyable as possible, as long as we finished the games, entertained, and won after 90 minutes. Our home crowd would vary between 1,500 to 2,000, and with Portsmouth FC literally just down the road, pulling in massive crowds at Fratton Park, our supporters were very loyal to us.

As a non-League club, we were also successful in winning the Hampshire Senior Cup, while doing very well in the FA Cup, getting to the first round proper. We played Wycombe Wanderers, who knocked us out, leaving us on catch-up, as all of the teams in the Southern League had played 23 or 24 games, while we had played only 17, because of our good cup runs, due to our strong squad. We paid the price when catching the teams above us. Barnet FC were promoted, while we finished fifth in the League.

In those days I found that players were not at clubs for the money, but to win trophies at all cost. Players then were at clubs to stay, and whether home or away, you got to make friends with the players marking you, after the 90 minutes. That is, yes, you respected players, there was no diving or arguing with the referee, unless it was a blatant challenge in the box. You generally accepted his decision, even if the supporters didn't. Systems were the same home or away, and you knew your jobs when you lost possession. If you didn't do them, your team mates, captain and all, not to mention some of our supporters made sure you knew, when we were at home. Dave Munks, our manager, was never a manager who screamed at his players, or ran up and down the touch line shouting at the referees and linesmen, as they were known back then. But in the dressing room prior to kick off he would explain to each and everyone their jobs with the ball, and when not in possession. Not forgetting we only had one player on the bench, Dave sorted out the changes if our goalkeeper was injured and who would drop in between the sticks, then the No 12 would go on in his place. Dave was very thorough when preparing us for 90 minutes, and at half time.

In those days the football language was straightforward: you had full backs who were defenders, and centre halves, one of whom was usually the Captain. There were usually four across the midfield, two wide wingers who got forward to deliver or beat the opponents' full backs and two up front, who were expected to score the goals or set a team mate up to score. Regarding set pieces, you had a player who could deliver or score if he could. Oh, and a good keeper who told his players constantly where they should be, during the 90 minutes, when we didn't have the ball and on corners and free kicks against. I realised during Jim Storrie's and Dave Munk's reign as managers that keeping players, once you felt you had a good squad for the first eleven, and a good reserve team, made life easier during training and games. I felt at that time, when Dave had taken over the squad from Jim Storrie, who had moved to manage St Johnstone, there was no need for changes in the team, therefore we all knew each other well enough to demand more on the pitch, whether in training or games. Only injuries to players meant we had to make changes, while we all knew our jobs. But we did know when a player took a bad knock in those days, none of this rolling and screaming we see nowadays. It's spoiling the games, and I feel for the officials. Assistant referees (linesmen) could give a lot more to help the refereee, so much so that this month (January 2018) they are going to have a camera looking at every aspect of the game in order for the referee to ask those who are watching the match on a TV link to view the incident, then explain to the referee the decision he should take. I'm sure it will be fine regarding the technical equipment they have today, but when in extra time, I hope the referee adds the time taken to sort out the findings of the camera crew. Will it help the game? We will have to wait and see.

Going back to Waterlooville, we were drawn against Hillingdon Borough FC in the fourth round of the Southern League Cup on Saturday 11th February 1978. We had played them on a couple of occasions. The game ended in a draw; no penalties in those days so we had to travel to Hillingdon on the Monday evening for a replay after a 1-1 draw at Jubilee Road, and they beat us 2-1 on the evening.

Our attendance at Jubilee Park was evidence that we were playing well, as our attendance for the home game against Chesham was 3,600. Regarding local derby games, Bognor Regis was about 28 miles away from Waterlooville. We were joint top of the Southern League South, with Margate, Dorchester, Aylesbury and us having 21 points each, so things were going well under Dave Munks.
While enjoying my football with Waterlooville, I kept my interest in St Johnstone and their results. Scotland is a friendly place, while the people are very competitive in what they do when it comes to sport. Nowadays the clubs in the Premier League and Championship

are always looking for players like Kenny Dalglish, Denis Law and Billy Bremner. Given that the population is only six million, they have had top sportsmen in football, rugby, tennis, boxing, swimming and athletics. They stay very loyal to that flag of Scotland, which is something I found during my spell at St Johnstone.

My prolonged stay at Waterlooville was I felt, going to last, as we were always up there with the leaders in the League and picking up silverware. I realised it was the mixture of good players who had a good attitude for the club. Losing a player and having to attend his funeral, soon after his accident on the pitch, was very rare. John Kill was out centre half alongside Alan Avery, our Captain. John had a large mole on his chest and during a League game at Jubilee Park, he was hit in the chest by the ball, which took the head off the mole and our physio couldn't stop the bleeding. John walked off with the physio, his shirt a deep red colour, while we prepared ourselves to continue the game once our substitute was on. At the close of the 90 minutes and a victory, all we were concerned about was John Kill. We learned in the dressing room that John had been taken to the Queen Alexandra Hospital. We heard from his wife that we could visit him on the Monday, so I, together with a few of the players went to see him. Things were different in those days; John had tubes and bandages everywhere, and though he was awake and carefully chatting to us, it wasn't difficult to see he was struggling. We stayed as long as the nurse allowed us, then as we left the ward, we chatted about John, saying he didn't look too good, but he was in the right place, and we would soon have him back in the side at centre back. Well, that was not to be; John passed away not long after, leaving us to attend his funeral along with dozens of family, players and supporters wanting to say goodbye to a truly treat lad and a very good footballer and friend.

Rest in peace, John, you are sadly missed by all.

Within a couple of weeks we brought Bobby Gill in to the centre half shirt and moved Paul Sexton to right back, and it worked, although Alan Avery and Bobby took a few games to learn about each other then, when they did, Richie Damerel broke his hand and while looking for a centre half, we needed a goalkeeper for the next couple of months. Trevor Gilbert came in for Richard and did a great job in goal. Richard had been Waterlooville's keeper since 1970: a quiet lad who you could rely on, who is still my friend today.

As I mentioned earlier, I felt that when the team rarely changed from one game to another, as players you got to know your team mates; they knew your flaws and your good points. It was only because of injuries that changes had to be made. You had to be aware, and information had to be passed on when under pressure, but was not always accepted. Still that's football!

Just phoned my best mate in South Shields. Shields are playing Hartlepool in the quarter final of the Durham Senior Cup. We went to Wembley to see Shields win the FA Vase, plus promotion to the Evostick North. The Chairman at South Shields has been amazing. Over the past three years, he has built a full-size G4 training area, and regarding the pitch, which is next to the training area, they have sorted out the indoor facilities, such as the changing rooms and the club bar and restaurant. They have also installed an under-soil sprinkler system; mind you they get enough rain in County Durham to keep the playing surface in good order for games! All the very best Mr Chairman!

Now, back nearer to home at the Ville. We made two new signings for the first team: Brian Bromley from Portsmouth, previously with Bolton Wanderers, who could play wide or in the midfield and Bobby Griggs, who previously played for Aldershot. Both proved to be very good signings; Brian was 31, very experienced and clever with the ball, while Bobby was very fit, only 24 years old, a very good defender, and very quick to match any No 9s and No 10s looking to get behind us. Also, both were good talkers on the pitch.

We did well in the FA Trophy, were in the top three in the League, and got to the semi-final of the Senior Cup.

In the 1979-80 season we made the signing of Hughie Fisher, an ex-Southampton player with 360 League games to his credit; a very funny and experienced footballer. He was another good asset to the club and a Scotsman. Couldn't go wrong! Our youngest players were Mickey Seymour (26) and Kim Manns (also 26) so we felt the side was very experienced and good enough to have a go at getting promotion.

At the end of January 1980 we had an away game at Aylesbury United FC. The two clubs were sixth and seventh in the League, with as many as six games in hand on Hillingdon FC who were top of the Southern League, with only six points between the Ville and them. The weather and cup games had made us lose ground on both Hillingdon and Dover, but we felt with our squad now established, we could give it a go. Going back a few seasons, we had signed Tommy Hare, a full back, who had also played for Southampton. Tommy, also Assistant Manager, sat us down before a game against Dorchester Town, away, and kept his pre-match speech to a few words, telling us, 'You get 90 minutes to lead by example, and if we all do that, the result will be our reward.' I have bumped into Tommy over the years that have passed and we have reminded each other of our previous games together. Although they are long past, some are very clear in our minds.

After doing quite well at the Ville and enjoying my football, I was given the option of joining Farnborough FC. Ted Pearce, the Manager, was down at Cams Hall, Fareham's ground, to watch the re-play of a cup game, and I saw him coming towards me. I knew him from my days in the Army at Aldershot. We spoke for about five minutes, with Ted asking me if I would like to join him at Farnborough. I told him I would give it some thought, not forgetting I was 32 years old. With that, he said, 'Maybe this will help. Open it when you get home, and read the terms. Also there is a signing-on amount in the envelope. If you do sign, you will receive the same cash amount when you become our centre forward.'

With that we watched the match then went on our ways. I said to him that he would receive my decision within 48 hours.

After giving it some thought while driving home, yet not having opened the envelope, I knew it could be a good move to finish my football. I had attained my coaching badges while serving in the Army, thus preparing me to coach and manage when my playing days were over. When I did get home, and indoors, I opened the envelope, took out the cash which was in there, and read the terms. John Waugh was Manager at Waterlooville at the time, and I wondered what his thoughts would be. I decided to speak to John before training on Thursday evening.

The following morning I rang John to explain. As he was a well-travelled football person, and coming from Lancashire, I knew him well enough to know that he would be straight with me. We chatted on the phone for a good 20 minutes and I said my thank yous for being honest with me. I took everything in, and decided to go to Peter Faulkner's house to chat to him, especially after what he had done for me and my family since signing for Waterlooville. I phoned Peter at his office, which was a short distance from Jubilee Park, knowing that he would be honest with me. I spoke to Peter in his office, going over me staying at the Ville, yet not putting pressure on me to stay at the Ville, and not mentioning what he and the club had done for me and my family, once. The talking was all based on football. Peter and John Waugh had helped in making my mind up. On arriving back home I chatted with Ann regarding the fors and against, then the decision was mine.

I decided to finish my footballing days at Farnborough and as far as finish, how true this was regarding my playing days. I signed for Farnborough, to the delight of Ted Pearce. The Chairman, Mr Richard Holden, became a close friend and was an excellent Chairman. Regarding the football, I enjoyed it. As long as I am playing I'm fine; yes, winning makes it better for everyone involved with the club, especially the supporters, but playing is where the love is with football, and scoring comes with the love.

My enjoyment and love for playing came to a halt one Saturday, some three months into my season with Farnborough, when I ruptured a muscle in my left thigh. The injury was not good and my recovery, just to get back to training, after rest and treatment, took almost four months. To get back to match fitness took another month in the reserves, and by then the Manager had to sign a replacement striker, which he did when told that my full recovery would take a while. As a club they looked after me, allowing me treatment near home, as driving was a dangerous venture. When I could drive comfortably, I drove to the physio's house in Fleet. As I had never had an injury as bad as this, I was told by all those who helped me through it, 'Do not rush your return, otherwise you could suffer a breakdown coming back too early.' During treatment, I couldn't even get up to watch my new club play, not being able to drive, and none of the players came from my area in Hampshire, so I became a spectator and supporter at Jubilee Road, watching my old club, Waterlooville, when at home. This was not something I enjoyed, supporting them on crutches. The time to recover and being given the green light to train with the first team at Farnborough took almost five months, yet I was still feeling a slight twinge when I went from jogging to sprinting. Did this mean more treatment?

After breaking down during more than training, I decided at this level I was being unfair to the staff and players, while receiving wages. I spoke to the Chairman and Ted Pearce, saying my thank yous for everything that they and Farnborough had done for me during my playing and recovery after injury. I knew how good football had been to me. My thoughts now were hopefully to go into coaching and managing, given that I gained my coaching badges while serving, or should I say playing football for the British Army XI, even while serving in Cyprus for months with the United Nations Peace-keeping Force, and enjoying helping 42 squadron RCT to the League championship, and winning the Island Cup in 1968. I came home after my six-month term was over and Ann was working in Lloyds Bank in Greenwich, and when I went to visit her, no one knew who I was, as in the photos I sent with my letters, I was always in football strip. Anyway, back to 1980, and kicking a ball for Farnborough had come to an end for me, and my thoughts were to stay in the game I loved, as a coach.

Coaching

After a while travelling to lots of matches in Hampshire, Sussex and Wiltshire, and helping a few friends on both Saturdays and midweek, I found that my injury was only bothering me after games. I kept myself fit by going out on runs and doing gym work.

A good friend of mine, Joe Laidlaw, had finished his professional career at Portsmouth, having had a great career playing for Middlesbrough, Carlisle, Doncaster Rovers and Mansfield. Having helped local non-League clubs, including Fareham and Waterlooville, he took over the Manager's job at Petersfield FC and asked me to join him as Assistant manager-coach, and player when required. Our partnership worked and Joe took us into the Vauxhall-Open League, after winning the Hampshire League. We also gained promotion to the Vauxhall League Division 2 South. Our first away game was against Hastings Town in the Gilbert Rice Floodlight Cup, which we lost. They were a good team and a couple of leagues above us. I felt that the travelling was becoming too much for Joe. He stepped down as manager the following week and I was asked to take over as manager. Well, here we go! Something I'd wanted to do after my playing days were over.

Not long had the word got round that I had left Steyning than I received a phone call from Alan Mullery, asking me to be the club coach, working alongside him. He obviously had not worked with non-League players after being a professional, and I felt he asked me to join him because of that. The partnership worked very well. I was learning from a pro-Manager and Alan was learning from someone who had been coaching non-League teams for a good while.

Alan hated the lame excuses for why the players had to give training a miss, or couldn't make a game, since he had to work on a Tuesday away from home. Consequently, the team was rarely the same. He found this difficult to accept after being a professional all of his footballing life. I learned a lot from Alan in the short time I worked with him. We rarely bumped into each other, yet one evening at the Marriot Hotel I attended an evening celebration for John Gregory's football career and Alan spotted me. He came over to chat prior to sitting on the top table, with John Gregory.

Managing

I managed Petersfield for a couple of seasons and realised, no matter what level you manage a club, that there is more to it than football knowledge. While I felt my football knowledge was OK, you also need to know your players, almost as well as their parents do. You have players who are listening but not taking what you have said onto the pitch, and you have leaders, both in the dressing room and on the pitch, whose will to win and lead their team mates through the game is very noticeable. They, providing they are good footballers at the level you are in, normally become your Captain.

Tuesdays and Thursdays in non-League are your training nights, which, as you all know, take up fitness and coaching. Early on in pre-season your players need to know they are going to work hard in preparation for friendlies before the season starts, and fitness is vital, in order that players can show you their talents and work rate. A manager's job is preparation and knowledge of his players. After three or four friendlies you need to know your starting eleven and your subs, to cover the loss of a player through injury and a player who the opposition have found to be a weak link, or change the system when you decide the way you have set your team up, be it home or away, isn't working. Also, your pre-match talk prior to the kick-off, not forgetting one voice only, should give them a lift and remind them we start with eleven players, and the referee is the boss out there.

I realise the laws and rules of the game change, but don't give the man in charge reasons for booking you or sending you off. Play to the rules and don't direct your feelings to him after you feel he has given a bad decision against your player, as this benefits the opposition. Direct all of your efforts into having a '7 out of 10' as they say, and you will come away with your team mates, happy you have done the right things for yourself, and the team, and the game you love. As players you don't ever play under the same manager for ten or twelve seasons, and no two managers are the same. Some you like and some you put up with, but when supporters pay to watch you and your team, you have to do your best for your club, your team mates, your supporters and yourself. We all know to do well receives the pats on the back, the headlines in the paper and the satisfaction you feel within yourself.

Bognor Regis FC 1981-82
In the 1981-82 season the very well-known Jack Pearce, who was managing Bognor Regis FC, asked me if I was fit enough to play for him, alongside Bob Musselwhite, up front. I said I would come over and do a few training sessions with the squad and see how both he and I felt. I got through the very hard sessions on the beach and found the squad he had were good players with good attitudes, so we both agreed to give it a go. Jack was very good to offer me a contract, given my age, and the possibility of my thigh injury reoccurring. The good thing was, I was playing 90 minutes OK.

I saw my contract out and can say that I really enjoyed my time playing alongside Bob Musselwhite and the rest of the squad. Jack climbed the footballing ladder and worked for the FA regarding all non-League matters. His brother Mick was also in football and worked alongside Jack. The players at Bognor were all good lads, which rubbed off from Jack as soon as they entered the club.

Managing/Coaching 1983-84

In the 1983-84 season Don Gowans asked me to join him at Eastleigh FC. We had worked together, when Don as managing the Hampshire youth team, but due to the fact it was a county youth team, we only got together every two or three weeks. Joining Eastleigh would be a good move, as training would be twice a week, with matches on Saturday, and some on Tuesday. This was what I needed. Eastleigh were a very forward-thinking club and well supported. Given the progress they have achieved to date, the club is now competing in the Vanarama National League.

Don used to prepare our training sessions, and would be present while we prepared the square. I would take the session, starting with the regular warm-up, then set out the players into the system we used, both home and away, given we had players who were flexible, and they knew if we altered the system during the 15 minutes of half time, we had prepared the squad. With Don's experience, and myself able to get involved as a player when required, the players were very respectful towards Don and me.

Due to the fact that our League finished earlier than the Northern League, I asked the club if we could take the squad up to my area in the North East to play a couple of friendly matches. I got in touch with Spennymoor FC and West Auckland FC and they agreed for us to travel and play both clubs. Due to the fact we had a good season, the board also agreed. With that, the players and I organised the trip. My sister organised the hotel up north, which meant it was on. We hired the coach and driver and were on our way.

None of our squad knew where Spennymoor or West Auckland were, so I decided to chat to them, telling them where and who the clubs were. When I told them about Spennymoor, with due respect, it didn't take long, but when I told them that West Auckland

40

had competed in the World Cup against the teams in Europe, and brought the cup home as winners in 1909, the only proof was to let them see the cup and hear the story when we played them. As it was, Spennymoor beat us 3-1 at the Brewery Field and invited our players and my family to their end-of-season presentation evening, something which didn't surprise me, coming from the area. We all had a fantastic evening and now looked forward to our game against West Auckland Town.

Two days later we travelled some six miles from our hotel to West Auckland, only to be told we couldn't play due to the state of the pitch following torrential rain over the past few days. However, the club had invited two elderly gentlemen to tell us the story about when their club had brought the World Cup trophy to West Auckland, lifting the trophy our of its case so we could take photos. What an excellent way to finish our trip to the North East. The following morning we set off back to Eastleigh, while chatting about our flying visit to the North East. Even to this day, when I bump into players from our trip, they always remind me of our time up north in 1983. Great Times! Which is what football allows.

Fareham Town FC 1984-85

After a very enjoyable time at Eastleigh I was asked by Roy Grant and Richie Reynolds to join Fareham Town F.C. as coach. I accepted the post feeling I still didn't have enough knowledge, or experience for managing. The club had always been well supported, and were ambitious. I joined Fareham Town hoping to help the club achieve some success. We had some very good players for the Southern League, and with Richie's experience as manager the future looked bright. Our biggest plus was signing Dave Leworthy, a centre forward, who the staff at Portsmouth FC didn't think was going to make it. I felt just the opposite; Dave was far too good for the Southern League, so I decided to phone up Bill Nicholson, Chairman at Tottenham Hotspur, a friend of mine through football. He said he would talk to the then Manager, Peter Shreeves. Peter Shreeves phoned me to ask me to bring Dave up for a pre-season friendly at Harrow Borough FC on the Tuesday evening, KO 7.45 pm. I phoned Dave to explain things. He was so grateful and really looking forward to it. On that Tuesday afternoon, Dave, his dad and his brother and

41

I drove to Harrow to be ready for the game. Peter Shreeves was a gentleman, as I introduced Dave and myself to him. He had already included Dave from the kick-off, up top, wearing the No 9 shirt. While feeling nervous for Dave, we felt he was good enough.

The referee blew the whistle for the off and within 20 minutes Dave had found the net three times for the Spurs' trialists. At half time Peter Shreeves asked Dave's dad and me into the boardroom at Harrow and said he wanted to sign Dave. He offered him a two-year contract, and an apartment not far from the training ground. Dave accepted all of the terms offered and became a Tottenham Hotspur first team squad player. Also, Fareham did well, as Spurs brought a team to Cams Alder, which had a few first team players on show, including Dave. Having picked up the programme for that occasion dated 10th September 1985, I read how Richie Reynolds was the person who organised Dave's move to Tottenham Hotspur. I could show you the photos of Dave in his Spurs strip, saying thank you for sorting out everything regarding his trial and his progress in professional football, but there have been no thank yous or mention in the programme from Fareham Town, whereas from Dave, I have more thank yous, photos and cards. It was a pleasure helping Dave to achieve the career he deserved. If you need to confirm this, then ask Dave himself.

I felt well pleased with Dave's ability on the pitch, and him being a perfect gentleman off it. Well done, 'Burger' – the nickname he gained from his team mates at Spurs. You had better ask Dave where that came from!

Player Manager Petersfield FC 1986-88

As mentioned earlier, my early days were spent working alongside Joe Laidlaw at Petersfield FC. Well after giving his all, Joe decided to take a rest, and John Stimpson and Dave Burnett asked if I would take over the manager's role, which I did, knowing the experience would do me good. After Joe's work and my limited knowledge as a manager, we managed to win the League and be promoted to the Vauxhall Opel League. Our first game was away to Hastings F.C. and as our players were only on expenses, the first team was a mixture of first and reserves, due to the fact that three or four of our first team squad could not leave work early. Needless to say we lost the game, and when finding out that our away matches midweek were all quite a distance away, we knew we would never be able to field a full side other than for a Saturday match at home. Both John and Dave tried to help financially, but it was just not working, so at the end of the season, we slipped back to the Hampshire League. I decided to step down, knowing we could not survive. I also stepped down from the job, knowing the club would only survive in the local League.

Player-coach at Steyning FC 1988-89

In 1988 I left Petersfield after learning a new job in management. Knowing every club can be very different regarding their outlook towards football, I was then asked by a friend Barry Youell if I would join him at Steyning FC in the Sussex First Division as a player-coach. I decided to help Barry out, knowing it would help me keep fit and involved. I enjoyed it apart from the travelling, especially on Tuesday evenings to away grounds in East Sussex.

I helped Barry for a few months, but once again the travelling took its toll, and I said to Barry and the players it was too much for me, as I was running my own plumbing and heating business, which took up lots of my time outside of football.

My small business consisted of myself, a fully qualified plumber, and an apprentice, so I had wages to find each week, along with trying to keep my books up to scratch, which my wife Ann kept on top of. Barry and the players and staff understood, so I left on good terms and still kept an eye on their results, as I knew it was the right thing to do at the time. If I received call-outs on Saturday, Ann always said I would be out on Sunday morning. Yes, I was my own boss, being a self-employed plumber and heating engineer. I explained to Barry that I was having to extend jobs, which I couldn't charge for, as the customers had accepted my estimate. As a businessman he understood.

My time in Sussex had to end, because the travelling was too much for me, running my plumbing business and juggling the time I needed to leave work, drive home, change into football gear for training, or shirt, trousers and jacket for a game.

After finding out that I had left Steyning, Chichester City FC asked me to join them. As I lived in Waterlooville, it was a 30-minute drive from my house to the club. I thought I could manage it three times a week, even if Tuesday was an away game.

My time at Chichester City was enough for me to refurbish the club and enjoy a short while on the pitch, but I knew I needed more, regarding my football. I needed to manage a club or be at least a coach for a club with ambition.

After helping out at various clubs as a coach and player, while I was still enjoying my football, I received a call from Alan Mullery, the Tottenham and England player, asking me to join him at Southwick as a coach, and if needed, a player. Alan had taken over from Ray McCarthy, who I had worked with, and also become very friendly with. Ray was a very good manager and demanded players show their worth. I remember our visit to Billericay Town in the Diadora League; I was on the bench. Billericay were third in the league, while we were second bottom, but Ray wasn't going to give away three points and he set the side out to attack, while the forwards and midfield players had to track back in front of our back four, who in turn did not drop off on to the 18-yard box if we lost possession. I felt each player knew Ray demanded a good work rate and fitness, or lack of it also showed, losing 4-0! I knew what was coming on Thursday evening training.

As it was, Ray set everyone down on the Thursday evening training and explained it was our fitness which lost us the game. As coach, I agreed and for the next few weeks we worked on fitness and stamina. A few weeks later Ray stepped down for personal reasons, and Alan Mullery took over as manager. After managing professional players, Alan found it difficult managing a non-League club, when training was Tuesday and Thursday; not enough time to maintain fitness and coaching, given four hours on the two evenings to prepare the first team squad for home and away matches.

While I picked up good points from both Ray and Alan, after three or four months Alan decided the non-League wasn't giving him enough time to prepare, coach and manage a team to success, so he stepped down as manager. I left also, finding the travelling tiring, and decided to look for a club and job which was nearer to home, as I knew the players in Hampshire and the clubs.

Coaching in the USA

I was still with Worthing FC when Gerry Armstrong was asked by the FA to get four coaches together to work in a summer camp at the University of Boston in the USA. I was excited when asked. Joe Craig and Darren Brown made up the four, including Gerry himself. When flying out to Boston we chatted on the plane, wondering what we were going to find regarding our work, but Gerry had only been given the University name and that a taxi would meet us at the airport. We would have the first summer camp influx of girls from Long Island in New York, giving us ten girls for each coach. We flew out on the Saturday, and the girls were arriving on Sunday afternoon ready for an introduction on Monday, then on with the coaching. We also had to make sure that in the evenings they were in their rooms by 9.30 pm, which included Sunday evening.

We arrived at our quarters in the University, picked our beds and made ourselves at home. Gerry had asked the taxi driver if there was anywhere near the campus that we could have a drink in the evenings. He told us that Charlie's Bar was just up the road from the campus gates.

We agreed to sort ourselves out, have a walk to Charlie's, then back for a good start when organising the girls coming in the next day, ready for a Monday start at 10 am. Charlie's Bar was fine, and when four new faces walked into the bar, every head turned. Gerry put all their minds at rest by saying to the lady behind the bar in his Irish accent, four half pints please; the lady lifted a glass and held it to Gerry, saying, 'This, fine?'

'Yes thanks,' Gerry replied, and that seemed to make us welcome. She poured us four drinks, asking, 'Are you here to work at the Uni for the summer camps?' Gerry replied yes to the question, saying we would be here for four weeks.
'We may see more of you over the next month,' she said, then asked our names. 'Gerry, Joe, Darren and Robbo.' 'Mine is Charlie,' the lady replied. 'Welcome.'

We got ourselves a table and all seemed fine. Not being a big drinker, my glass was still half full, and three halves were delivered. After two hours of relaxing, we decided an early night was the answer, given we did not know how tomorrow was going to pan out. On the walk back Joe said, 'We will pick straws to see who is on duty tomorrow.' We did, and Joe ended up doing the first night.

Given that football was still growing in the States, we decided the basics of football would take up the first two or three days, not forgetting 'a scrimmage' was a game between two sides after training and coaching, and 'cleats' were boots. It seemed we had a lot to learn before we taught the girls.

Sunday afternoon 2 pm, a coach arrived, as did our 40 girls. They seemed to congregate en masse, so we asked them to get into four groups of ten, the age groups being correct in the four groups, i.e. 12, 13, 14 and 15-year-olds. After approximately 15 minutes we finally had our four groups. We did say, 'Prior to us knowing your names, we will do our best to get each one of your names right in our group come the end of the week. Also ladies, you will be in your rooms by 9.30 pm, with lights out by 10 pm. The early call in the morning will be 8 am. Breakfast will be between 8.30 and 9 am in the restaurant, with a 10 am start for your coaching on the training facility's pitches.' Given they knew the times we had been told that all the balls, cones, flags, etc. would be ready for us in the coaches' training rooms. The final thing to explain to the girls was that they were not allowed off the campus for the six days they were here, and on Saturday morning they would show their parents what progress they had made over the six days, prior to leaving the campus. 'Lunch is 1 to 1.30 pm and your evening meal is 6 pm unless you decide to come out for an organised game, 7 to 8.30 pm. We will see how things work out, and that will be up to you all.'

Sunday evening, it was up to Joe to make sure all was well by 9.30 pm then back at 10 pm to turn the lights out. When he got back, he told us all seemed fine, just some giggling, but no real problems.

'That's good,' Gerry said. I'm sure he felt responsible for us all, including the girls. The morning came round and we were making for the restaurant for breakfast. Now Brandeis University was a Jewish University, so we had to respect their rules and religion. All seemed fine and we all congregated on the sports facility's grounds, finding everything we needed and more, neatly on benches and hangers, and the soccer balls in bags of ten balls.

We decided after each group had formed, that to warm up before kicking a ball is most important, to hopefully keep them free of any injuries, also when warmed up, players are shown stretching exercises, which we hope they will carry out before kicking a ball or sprinting. I was amazed at my group, yes, they were 15-year-olds, but still listened and did exactly what was asked of them. Honestly, there was no messing about, so on with the coaching.

The first week went very well; no injuries, just 40 girls enjoying football, and doing very well with, or without, the ball. On our final session on Friday we practised with the ball what we were going to do for their parents and friends, to let them see the progress they had made. My girls were last as they were the oldest group, so I took them on a warm-up while the other groups were performing their skills on what they had learned. After each group performed, their coach had to sum up their group's progress to the parents, according to his assessment. I was last with my group. My girls put on a really good performance, leaving me to sum up. 'Excellent' I said.

We all felt that the 40 girls were a pleasure to get to know and work with; the only problem I had, with Sara, was I had to 'knock her up' every morning for her to be ready for coaching. The crowd who had been applauding when Gerry, Joe and Darren summed up their girls, went deathly quiet, and Sara's parents were white. Her father walked towards me to explain what I had just said, and what it meant. I then apologised and explained to everyone just what I meant. Sighs of relief and a few hands clapping helped the crowd to laugh, prior to Gerry summing up our first week. When I thanked my group for their hard work and enjoyment in learning and said my cheerios I decided to apologise again to Sara's mum and dad. Her mum said their thank yous, then looking at Sara said, 'You were right, she doesn't like to get up in the morning.'

That evening the boys and I walked up to Charlie's for a drink and discussion about our first week's work. I don't need to explain the main topic. But at least now I know what to say, and what not. 'Sorry Sara!'

USA 1993
I had travelled to Boston USA with Gerry Armstrong, Northern

Ireland and Watford; Joe Craig, ex-Celtic and Blackburn Rovers; Darren Brown, Worthing FC; and myself, an Army international and St Johnstone. We worked for the world-class soccer camp, as organised by the FA. The requirements were you had to have your FA coaching badges, and have played and coached at a good level. Our base was Brandeis University. What a terrific experience! We were looked after and well paid. We were invited back the following year, for the same work (if you could call it work).

During our second term in Boston, on our three days off after taking the girls we were coaching back to Long Island, New York in a 16-seater minibus we had hired, we carried on to Donald Trump's Atlantic City to spend our money in the casino. By the way, Gerry was driving.

We arrived at the casino and were given directions to the parking area. As you probably know, in 1994 America was still like us, in feet and inches. Gerry drove to where we were told to park the minibus, and turned into a multi-storey parking area. As we entered, a sign in front of us said, 'maximum height 5 feet 10 inches.' With that, Gerry turned to me and asked, 'Robbo, are we higher than 5 feet 10 inches?'

So I said, 'Give me a tape measure and I will tell you,' which obviously none of us had. Anyway, Gerry, being Gerry, drove up hoping to get under the 5 feet 10 inch girder, which we realised when we came to a halt under the girder, was stuck inside a badly damaged minibus. Not knowing what to do, we stepped out of our minibus, holding up the cars behind us with people who had come to Atlantic City to enjoy an evening's gambling. We scratched our heads wondering what to do with a badly damaged bus holding up six or seven cars. One of the guys in a chauffeur-driven limo got out of his car, came up to us and said, 'Let the tyres down, drive up to the next level, park the bus, take the keys to the parking reception, explain everything that has happened, and they will take care of it all.' With that, we let the tyres down, got back into the bus and crawled up to the next parking level. Gerry, with us backing him, went to the parking office, put the keys on the desk and explained our problems to the guy in charge. He then realised we were British, and said, 'You guys go and enjoy your evening and we will see what we can do.' Off we went into the casino, thinking about the minibus and wondering.

Joe Craig and I had discussed our visit to Atlantic City and decided we would take $1,000 each to spend, saying, 'That should be enough,' after explaining to each other that neither of us knew the first thing about spinning the wheel, or Blackjack; anyway, into the casino we went. We watched for about 20 minutes, trying to pick up hints from people playing the different tables. Then, as experts, we changed our dollars for chips. We stood and looked at our money, which had now turned into colourful plastic coins with numbers on them. We had also agreed that whoever won between the two of us, the other would get half of the winnings. Twenty minutes into our gambling spree, we had lost $2,800 or £2,000. We looked at each other and Joe said, 'Ah, it's only money Robbo!'

I agreed, then said, 'Neither of us has anything, it's a good job the drinks are free.' With that, we decided to find Gerry. We found our friend playing the one-armed bandits, and he was winning. The money was in the tray of the machine he was playing and lots of it!

'Hi, guys,' he said, 'How are you doing?' 'Not as well as you,' said Joe. 'Why, what's up?' 'We played the tables,' Joe said. With that the little light on his machine came on and more money filled the tray with his winnings. Joe and I left Gerry to count his winnings while people watched at the different tables.

You forget the time in a place full of money and wealth, and as it was approximately 2 am, we got together and decided to go back to our university digs in Boston. Sure enough, we picked up our keys from the parking office and the bus was ready for the road, apart from the big dent on the front roof. We said our thank yous and Gerry gave the guy $50 for his trouble. On we got and set off for Waltham, in Boston, not knowing what was going to happen regarding our damaged minibus. Gerry carried on driving home and we chatted about our visit to Atlantic City. He laughed when I told him about Joe and me losing two grand in 20 minutes.

'I managed to win,' he said. 'Good,' I said, thinking about the cost to repair the minibus. His answer was a question to me. 'You know George Best, Robbo?' 'Yes,' I said, 'as a friend, as well as a footballer.'

'I have invited George to the university to introduce him to the new intake on Monday.' 'Great!' I said, 'What a good idea!' 'He is meeting us today, Sunday for a night out, then staying over for tomorrow.'

With that, Gerry pulled in near a phone kiosk. The lads and I wondered who he was phoning. Anyway, we soon arrived at the minibus offices, but Gerry parked the minibus as far away from the office as possible. Out we got, only to see George Best standing by a taxi. Gerry shouted him over, saying to us, 'George is a massive personality in the USA, as big as Pele.'

Anyway, into the office we walked and put the keys and paperwork on one of the desks. With George standing next to him, Gerry said, 'Hey guys, it's George Best!' With that, Joe Craig, Darren Brown and I said our thank yous to the staff, walked out and hailed a taxi.

Back at the uni, we sat in the lounge of our digs, tired but waiting for George and Gerry. Thirty minutes later, in they walked. 'How did it go regarding the damage to the bus?'

'No problem,' Gerry said, 'They were all too busy wanting autographs and photos of George to even send anyone to make sure the minibus was OK.' George stayed over, and when we introduced him to the new intake, they all knew of him, so the photos and autographs were a must! George took it all in his stride, and we had a great evening at Charlie's Bar, where he seemed to be wanted by everyone. What a great guy!

Worthing Town FC 1991-94
Not long after preparing myself to leave Steyning, I received a call from Gerry Armstrong, the Northern Irish International. He had just taken over the manager's job at Worthing FC and wanted me to take the coaching job alongside him there. He asked me to drive down on a Monday evening to Woodside Road in Worthing to meet himself and the Chairman, Beau Reynolds. I agreed out of good manners, explaining where I lived and that traffic permitting I would aim for 7 to 7.15 pm and arrived at the Woodside Road ground on time. Gerry told me he had good reports from the clubs I had worked for and that I had managed to pick up a few trophies on the way.

After listening to both Gerry and Beau, and looking at the facilities,

I realised their plans for the club were substantial and capable regarding the Woodside Road ground. Gerry asked me about the players who had impressed me during my time in Sussex.

'Yes, there were a few,' I said, 'but are you looking to change the team?' 'No,' said Gerry, 'but when we see what we need you can advise me, and we can get them in. While our players are good, we will need to know early on if they are good enough to win the League, giving us the promotion to suit the proposed facilities we are looking to improve.'

Gerry then turned to Beau and said, 'I will leave you two to discuss the finances with John for this season.'

For some reason, I wasn't going to mind how much Beau Reynolds was going to pay me, as long as I covered my expenses going back and forth to Worthing and to away games. I've not had any worries as long as I'm not out of pocket.

I then joined Gerry, with Beau in the bar for a drink. 'What are you having John?' said Gerry, as if he knew I would be joining Worthing with him. 'A coke please, Gerry, no ice.' 'Two whiskies and a coke, please, no ice.'

Then he offered his hand for me to shake, saying, 'Welcome to Worthing Town John, or is it Robbo?' I shook his hand and said, 'Yes, Robbo is fine.' He said 'It's not for me, it's for the company who will make your kit for training etc.' I knew then I had done the right thing in agreeing to sign for a season.

The following evening was training and Gerry added, 'Training starts at 7.30 pm, not here, but we all meet at the club, change and then in cars we go to our training area, approximately two miles up the road. Once everyone has been there for the first two or three sessions, then we will meet there and our kit man will take what we need and we can all go direct, and when we have finished, it's back to the club for showers and a chat with the players. Can you take the session tomorrow Robbo? I know it's only 24 hours away, but I'm sure you are capable and it will allow you to get to know the lads.'

'Yes, no problem, but I will phone you tomorrow and explain my session, as I need to know what they have been doing pre-season.'

'Yes, give me a ring about midday and run it by me.'

I rang Gerry as promised and I explained what I would be doing. He said, 'Make sure you allow time for a kick-about for 20 minutes at the end of your session.'

The lads would soon tell you if you don't organise a six or seven-a-side kick-about after a session. My session was to last approximately 45 minutes on warm-up, then short bursts of sprinting and changing direction, etc. No balls until that was finished, then an exercise I do with all outfield players, while allowing our two goalkeepers to use the ball in the goal from both long crosses into the box and short shot-saving from the 18-yard area, allowing two players to help in their practice.

When that is done, after 45 minutes, no matter who you are taking, regarding non-League players, you will always get the remarks, 'Are we going to get the balls out? It will be dark soon.' Well, not knowing the boys, but knowing it's always about getting the balls out, I shared the bibs out, put one goalkeeper in one goal and the other in his team's goal and asked them to make sure we had two forwards up front, with four across the middle and four at the back, and I would be the referee. Let me tell you, after 15 minutes each way I was very impressed with most of the session and most of Worthing Town players had given their all. This may have been because I was new, or maybe Gerry had a word with them, but I was impressed.

I worked alongside Gerry, and for the Chairman, Beau Reynolds, for some three seasons, during which time the club did really well, gaining promotion to the new Diadora League, and winning the Sussex Floodlit Cup. Then just out of the blue, Gerry was offered the Manager's job for Northern Ireland's International team for the 1994 season, to which he said yes, as long as I was promoted to manage Worthing Town in his place. Since I had worked at the club for the previous three seasons as Gerry's coach, the Chairman agreed and I became Manager.

'Thanks Gerry and all the very best in your new job,' was my phone call after Beau Reynolds had told the press of Gerry's appointment.

As the new season was almost upon us, Beau received a request from the FA regarding changing the rules about the ball going out of play. He agreed with the FA and the BBC that they could visit the club and televise our attempt, showing kick-ins as opposed to throw-ins from the by-line. I ran this by the players and the staff, and as expected, some of the players were against it. Some said, 'Maybe it could work,' and the staff and I realised we would need to practise it, as the TV cameras would be there, therefore we couldn't keep making mistakes, and hearing a voice shout, 'We need to do that again, please.'

When we got it right, I, like most of the players, was undecided, but could see that it could work, especially when the attacking team had a kick-in in line with the opponents' 18-yard box. It became as good as a corner for the attacking team. After a good 30 minutes of playing, and practising this new possibility, the FA representative took the film from the BBC guys, saying thank you for what we had done, and left Woodside Road. The chap who was asking the players what their views were then came to me sitting in the stand and looking over what we had been doing regarding a possible FA rule change. My answer was that there were fors and againsts changing the rules, but I could see it slowing the game down, as when you were given a kick-in, in the attacking area on the pitch, do you take a quick kick-in or do you wait for your big defenders to come up for the ball into the box for a goal-scoring chance, leaving a defender back just in case? He summed it up in a few short words, saying, 'It's the same for both teams.' He was correct, but the FA decided not to go ahead with the change. By the way, I often wonder how it would change the game. We will never know, but thanks for choosing Worthing Town FC for the privilege.

Leading up to being offered the Northern Ireland Manager's job, Gerry Armstrong had done a very good job at Worthing, and I had enjoyed coaching and working alongside him, while picking up from his experience. It was the same with Alan Mullery. They were ex-professional internationals, very down-to-earth, and respected the game, which gave them both the success they deserved, yet were willing to start at non-League football, learn their managerial trade at the lower standard, and work their way up. Alan was at Brighton-and-Hove Albion, and Gerry was manager for his country. You don't get much better than that. How lucky was I! 'Thank you both.'

Prior to my three seasons working with Gerry, and then taking the manager's job at Worthing, the Chairman, Beau Reynolds, who had become a good friend of mine, explained that if I felt we needed to change things, either on the pitch or off it, I was to come to him first and discuss what I thought would make the team and the club more prominent in both Sussex and the Diadora Football League. Gerry Armstrong had done a very good job, winning promotion to Division 1, now it was up to Jimmy Quinn and me, my player-coach, to take us forward, hopefully into the Diadora Premier League.

Beau Reynolds had decided to change things regarding giving a bonus payment for a win, on top of the team's weekly expenses, which the players would receive at the end of the season, given that we won promotion. This was the 1994-95 season. The season started off well and we soon found ourselves in the top five at the turn of the year, hoping we could push for promotion come the end of the season. Prior to our final game, Beau asked me to arrange a meeting with the footballing staff and players in the Woodside Road bar to discuss the fact that we had gained promotion to the Premier League. Our final game was away at Abingdon Town near Oxford. Beau had organised a coach to Abingdon and he would pay the players their bonus on one condition, that all players and staff would attend the match in full fancy dress, otherwise no bonus would be paid out. Also, all those in fancy dress had to be recognisable as a celebrity of the time, male or female.

Early on the Saturday, we were all to meet at Worthing, as Beau had booked a hotel near Worthing railway station on Saturday evening for all of the staff and players. Our goalkeeper for the final game was Jason White ('Knocker' to all at the club), who at the time was living with his wife in London. He asked Beau if he could drive to Abingdon on Saturday, then follow the coach back to Worthing for the celebrations. Given the circumstances Beau agreed, but he must come in full fancy dress. 'Knocker' was a naval marine, covered in tattoos on both arms and legs. I assure you, you will not believe what I am going to tell you happened to Jason 'Knocker' White that weekend.

I myself went as Rab C Nesbitt. Steve Riley, the team Captain, was Jock Mac Jock in a kilt, braces, clown's feet and a tam o'shanter hat. We had Elvis Presley (Richard Tiltman), Darren Hewitt was a caveman, Darren Robson was Rod Hull, Jimmy Quinn was Winston Churchill.

On Saturday 23rd April, our coach pulled into the car park, and was led to the parking area for coaches, where we all grabbed our bags. One by one we stepped off the coach and made our way to the dressing rooms. As we got to the entrance, the groundsman showed us to the away dressing-room. Smiling as we walked past him he commented on our fancy dress, guessing who was who as we squeezed past him. He then turned around and asked, 'Why the fancy, boys?' So we said that as we had gained promotion, our chairman would treat us to a celebration weekend, providing we attended the game in full fancy dress. He then said, 'Is there a prize for the best fancy dressed celebrity?'

'Not as we know, unless our chairman picks someone.' 'Well, he said, 'in my opinion, you are all recognisable as the characters you depict, but the winner for me, would be your player who is already in the dressing room.' 'Why?' we all asked. 'Wait and see for yourselves.'

We couldn't wait to see who Jason 'Knocker' White had come as, but even as we guessed, we would never have been correct. In the corner of the away dressing room, sitting under the goalkeeper's peg, was Madonna dressed in a white pointed bra, a short, and I mean short, white skirt, black nylons, high heels, and nothing else other than Jason's tattoos. Well, we all fell about laughing, then clapping, as he had travelled from London to Abingdon in Oxford, dressed as Madonna. The laughter and questions went on for about 15 minutes. I felt guilty having to calm things down, as we had a game to play. With that, our kit man had arrived with our physio, Jack Anderson, to prepare us for our usual warm-up exercises, and they enjoyed what they saw, guessing who was who, until they looked at Jason, not knowing whether to give him his rub down, or ask him for a date. Trying to get some attention from the players was impossible, so as quickly as I could, I got the lads out onto the pitch. The mood regarding the squad was fantastic. I realised nothing I was going to say was going to change things, so much so, they were calling each other by their fancy dress names. Back in the dressing room, I left the pre-match chat to Jimmy Quinn, our midfield general, but the quips were coming out, no matter what Jimmy said, so out we went, not really prepared as footballers should be. However Beau Reynolds, made his usual walk onto the pitch, to talk to the players, and surprisingly, the players calmed down. I don't know what he said, but it worked. He came off to tell me that he had explained the fancy dress situation to Abingdon's Chairman, so he could pass it on to his manager and staff.

It was a good game, which we drew with no injuries or problems, and when we showered and dressed, the fancy dress outfits took a back seat, as we changed into shirts, trousers and shoes, apart from one player, yes, Jason 'Knocker' White, our goalkeeper. When he changed and dressed he was still Madonna. He thought the fancy dress was for the weekend.

We then went into the club house at Abingdon for our after-match eats, and the odd drink, with Jason 'Knocker' in his fancy dress. It took a while, with everyone wondering why, as they knew who he was dressed up as. After a couple of sandwiches and a drink, Jason 'Knocker' stood up and said to us, 'Right guys, I'm off, see you at Worthing,' and off he went.

It gave us a chance to tell everyone why the fancy dress, and that he had driven up from London, while we had come on the bus from Worthing, and our fancy dress outfits were back on the bus.

We sat with the opposition players, then after about 30 minutes or so Beau Reynolds asked us if we were ready to leave, so up we got, said our cheerios and got on the bus for the journey back to Worthing.

After approximately 30 minutes on the road back, a few of the lads thought they noticed Jason's car on the side of the road, parked and empty. Anyway, the driver just carried on, then, after a few hundred yards, there was Jason, thumbing a lift in his fancy dress.

I said to the driver, 'Drive on, don't stop,' while the players were doing moonies out of the back window. I then said to the driver, 'Drive on until we can turn around, then go back and get him.'

After a few miles we managed to turn around and as we passed him, he was still thumbing a lift, as Madonna. The driver looked for an opening to do a U-turn, and we stopped and picked him up.

'What happened?' we asked, as we all applauded him onto the bus.

'My car broke down, so I just left it on the side of the road.' 'So where are your clothes?' 'I didn't bring any, because I thought we were supposed to stay in fancy dress for the weekend.'

Anyway, we were too busy laughing, thinking, only Jason 'Knocker' would think we were staying in our fancy dress for the weekend, and only Jason would come in fancy dress as Madonna.

As we arrived in Worthing, Beau Reynolds stood in the coach and explained he had booked us into a hotel for the night, then handed out our bonus envelopes, saying, 'Thank you for a great season.' We all said our thank yous to our brilliant Chairman and friend, then made our way to our rooms in the hotel, explaining to the receptionist why one of our players was dressed as Madonna. She laughed as she handed us our room keys. We didn't know until we came down from our rooms, that Jason had nothing else to wear for our evening's celebration in the town. The only person who didn't seem to worry was, yes, you guessed, Jason 'Madonna' White, or as we knew him, 'Knocker' White.

I can honestly say that Knocker made the evening just as we expected, even though one of the clubs we went to wouldn't at first let us in. The two doormen, or bouncers, said he wasn't appropriately dressed, however after explaining who we were, and that he would not cause any trouble, in we went. Inside the music and the people added to a great evening with 'Madonna' giving everyone something to laugh about, coming over to him just to have a closer look. I ask you, when you read this, how many people could go through breaking down in their car, leaving it at the roadside, then walk, thumbing a lift, knowing what you were wearing was your dress for the next 48 hours? Then going out with friends to celebrate and being the centre of attention, due to wearing fancy dress? No-one, is the answer. Well, to finish this true episode of Jason's amazing weekend, on Sunday morning we all agreed to meet in the dining hall of the hotel at 9.30 for breakfast and say our goodbyes, as the season was finished, promotion was achieved and I would be in touch for pre-season training and matches in

July, preparing for the oncoming season. Give or take five minutes either side of 9.30 we all met in the dining hall for breakfast, along with Jason, 'Knocker', or better still 'Madonna'. As he walked in, you could hear a pin drop. Being Jason, he went over to the food area and chose his breakfast food, sat down with us, and chatted about our weekend over a cup of tea. On finishing his breakfast, we asked, 'How are you getting home to London?' 'By train,' he said.

The next train to London was 10.20. We all looked at each other, knowing he wasn't joking. There we were, with our Madonna, ready to see him off on what was going to be, for him, a journey where he was going to be the centre of attention, and what stories would be told to friends and relations when they arrived home! How many would believe them when they told those friends and relations? Well, I can honestly say, every word is true, and anyone who knows Jason White, our goalkeeper, and ex-Royal Marine, knows it is true. What an amazing man, when he is Madonna! Thanks Knocker, take care mate!

During 1990 to 96 seasons at Worthing Town I enjoyed every minute, both as coach to Gerry Armstrong and then as manager, with Jimmy Quinn as my player-coach. Beau Reynolds, Chairman, Morty Hollis who was President, Jack Anderson our physio, and the staff and supporters who had been playing a big part in Worthing's success over the past ten years, allowing the players at all levels to be confident that they were playing for a well-run football club, whose ambitions were clear to see, both on and off the pitch.

Yes, you play to be as successful as you can, to win trophies and gain promotion to the next level, for your players, the staff and the club, yet sometimes you forget the people who keep your club going from week to week financially. They love their football, especially when their club is doing well, but the players, coaches and manager take the plaudits, week in and week out when you are winning, or gaining a point against a side who are up there with you in the league. Then think of the Chairman and his Directors, and a handshake along with thank you doesn't go amiss.

I remember when we reached the first round proper in the FA Cup, and were drawn against Bournemouth AFC. at their ground. The players and the staff knew we had done well to get to the first round proper, and we knew that being away to a league team we had to be at our best. We prepared as usual, knowing we had to measure their fitness against ours. On our Thursday night training prior to our game against Bournemouth, the Chairman had arranged a meeting in the club house with everyone involved in Saturday's FA Cup. He said he would come into the dressing room before the kick-off, but to ask us to bring wives and girlfriends, as he had booked us all into the Moat House for a celebration evening, and also he had booked the buses to bring the supporters to the game, and home afterwards.

We lost to Bournemouth 3-1 after taking the lead from a corner by Spencer Mintram, which found the net without anyone touching the ball. In the end, they were fitter and better with the ball, although we gave it our all, making a good impression for a club some six leagues below them. I reminded the players on the way back to Worthing that Beau Reynolds, our Chairman, had paid for everything, even the supporters' coaches, and his reward was to see his club play against Bournemouth in the FA Cup on the 12th November of the 94-95 season. I can honestly say, during my five seasons at Worthing, as coach and as manager, myself, the players and the staff at all levels were given everything required to allow us success in our desire and ambition to succeed.

Thank you, Mr Chairman, on behalf of our players, our staff and our supporters during my time at Worthing Town FC, for everything. RIP Beau Reynolds.

Under Gerry Armstrong we were the 92-93 Division 2 Champions, plus winners of the Sussex Floodlit Cup. Gerry then left to manage the Northern Ireland national team. I took over as Manager at the beginning of the 94-95 season, when we were promoted to the Diadora Premier League and won the Sussex Floodlit Cup again. Also as mentioned, we reached the first round proper of the FA Cup.

Hampshire Youth Coach - 1996-97
On my return to Hampshire, Roy Beasley, who was Manager of the Hampshire Senior Youth Team, asked me to work with him as the coach. I didn't know many of the youth players, however I saw this as a good move, knowing that in a season or two, I might get a manager's job, when these young players would have some

more experience, and knowing them would allow me to approach their club and hopefully sign them, knowing how and where they could do a job for the club. I knew Roy well, and working alongside someone with his experience would be a plus for me, as I had mostly worked with older players, and young lads don't want to respond if you are constantly shouting at them when they make mistakes.

It didn't take me long, listening to Roy explaining to the lads how and when they could have done better for the team. His approach rubbed off on me, even though I was a fully qualified FA coach; you are never too old to learn. We played local youth teams from the New Forest and in the Portsmouth area and attended youth matches to make sure that we had not missed any quality injured players, or lads who were on holiday, in preparation for the Senior Youth County Championship. It took two or three trial matches after we had pencilled in the players we had agreed. Then, once we were clear regarding our squad of 18, we also had to alert clubs and players as to their availability when we entered competition mode.

To say that I also enjoyed my work with the Hampshire youth side is very much under-stated. Week in and week out we watched the progress of young players who obviously loved their football and were keen to better their game, which made it a pleasure to work with them, both individually and as part of the team. Once we had selected our squad and named our starting line-up, we played our first game at home in the Youth County Championship, from where we progressed to the quarter-final, where we travelled to Worcester to play on Kidderminster's ground. Sadly, we lost. They had a young lad who played in midfield who was the stand-out player for two reasons. First of all, he was a very gifted creator in their midfield and secondly, he only had one arm. We lost 2-1, and after the game I spoke to their manager, asking him about the young lad in the midfield who literally ran the game for Worcester.

Everyone talked about him during and after games, mostly about having only one arm, yet being such a good player. He just let his ability do the talking, yet he never complained about his disability, he just loved football.

Until now, May 2018, I've only spoken about the lad on a couple of occasions, but what an example he would show these so-called professionals, when they dive and roll about as if Anthony Joshua had hit them with a right hook. What an example he would be! I hope the lad had a good career playing the game he loved. I'm sorry, but unusually for me, I didn't pick up a programme, therefore I don't know his name, but I will not forget the ability and the love for football he showed, during and after the game, when congratulating our players on a very good game.

I thanked the players and staff, but my final and most important one is to Roy Beasley for the belief and respect he gave me.

We felt for Roy, and how much he is missed, 'Gone but never forgotten. RIP Roy Beasley MBE.' The church near St. Mary's was full with family, footballers and friends, to say cheerio to a lovely man in every sense of the word.

Alton Town FC 1998-2001
After a reasonable success with the Hampshire Youth Team, working with Roy, Jim McKell, Chairman of Alton Town F.C., offered me the manager's job, starting at pre-season 1998. I drove to the football ground, which was part of the Bass brewery land, hence the club was known as Bass Alton. I was to work with Vic Powell as joint manager. Some of the players at the club I knew quite well, and those I didn't know in football, I felt had the making of a good squad. Vic didn't stay long after I had joined, as he was travelling miles three times a week. He was a good chap to work with, but the travelling was not helping him, so he decided to step down.

I appointed Hughie Doyle, an ex-Navy man and friend. His main important subject when mentioning the clubs, was that he supported Manchester City. Hughie knew I was a Sunderland supporter, then, and still am now. We still see each other and he has great delight in telling me about Man City. They are a great club, under Pep Guardiola, yet Sunderland are relegated again. Anyway, our work was with Alton Town, so we gave it our best.

At the end of a very good season with Alton Town we, as a club, won the Hampshire League with a record number of points, hopefully gaining promotion to the Wessex League. However, when the Wessex League officials came to the club to inspect the ground and facilities, their report outlined the problems that required updating. Those requirements meant that they could not allow us promotion into the Wessex League. After gathering the players, staff and directors, our Chairman explained what needed doing to bring the amenities up to standard and the safety standards that needed to be updated. Given that the finance within the club could not cover the work needed, it left no alternative but to look elsewhere for our football for the new season.

Camberley had previously asked me if I would meet with their Chairman, Ian Waldren, and since we agreed on most things regarding the club and football, I accepted the manager's job and took Hughie Doyle with me, after our success at Alton Town. We organised a few pre-season friendlies against Tadley and Basingstoke, only to find four of my Alton Town players wanted to join me at Camberley Town. This was very pleasing to both Hughie and myself, when Nicky Guy, a very good defender, Clive Ventham, my captain at Alton, and a very good midfield general, Micky Street, another big strong defender, and Martin Whiddett, a goal-scoring centre forward, joined Camberley Town. Ian Waldren was a good chairman, and Ken Weaver, our physio, was always ahead of the play, reacting to each and every one of our players when needed. We took Ken's word when he explained the fitness of players recovering from injuries.

Once the players had been put through pre-season training and friendlies and were ready for the start of the 1999-2000 season, we got off to a reasonable start. Noticing our goalkeeper, Justin Grey, was being asked to do a lot more as a keeper than expected, we decided to incorporate a sweeper-type centre half, who controlled the players in and around him when we were under pressure, and with Graham Green and Clive Ventham, one had to drop into the back line, keeping four and a sweeper. Yes, we felt it was a defensive move, but away from home against teams like Croydon, Aveley and Hornchurch, etc., it worked. We ended up in the top half of the season and reached the final of the Aldershot Cup. I felt it was OK, but without the boys from Alton joining us, that might not have been the case.

Hughie and I were talking after driving home from the end of season presentation, wondering if we could get the players who had joined us at Camberley Town back at Alton Town to strengthen the squad. Between us we could carry out the requirements needed at Anstey Road and go for promotion again. Yes, we knew it was a tall order, but if we all turned up and got stuck in, then anything was possible.

We all worked together, while the necessary materials were supplied by Jim McKell, Reg Smith and others. The work required was carried out, and all we had to do when the season finished was apply for promotion, if we finished first or second. It was a very good season both in the League and the Hampshire Senior Cup, giving us the promotion we needed and a good run in the cups. Following a visit from the gentlemen to inspect our ground and its safety needs, we were given the thumbs up, and we were promoted into the Sydenhams Wessex League Division One.

Winchester City FC 2002-03
Mr Malone asked me to take over the Manager's job at Winchester City FC, as we had won the final game against his team 3-0 the previuos season. I decided, given the terms, to accept the job.
My next job was to appoint someone to work with me, who was experienced and knew the game, such as Hughie Doyle, whom I had worked with at previous clubs. But he couldn't commit to a season at Winchester City, due to his work commitments. With that, I phoned Neil Hards, an ex-professional goalkeeper, to ask him to join me. Neil invited me to his house for a chat, before making a decision. After our chat over two or three cups of tea, Neil agreed to join me at Winchester, and after listening to his knowledge regarding football and players in general, I knew he would be good to work with, however Mr Malone, the Chairman, wasn't so easy to work with, as I found out later in the season.
Neil and I put together a squad and after a few pre-season games. We both felt comfortable with the players we had brought in and the bench we had were capable of replacing any player who had to come off through an injury or looked to have heavy legs.

I was given my contract, signed by myself and Mr Malone, but once again I didn't read it, as all I was interested in was winning games with our players, both in League and Cup matches, and Neil and I felt we had a very good squad for success.

We had a very good start in the League, unbeaten after eleven games in the Hampshire Premier League, scoring 47 goals and conceding only five. We were to go on to win the FA Vase, playing the final at Birmingham's ground; we also won the Wessex League, and we won the Wessex League Cup.

Yet prior to our final in the Vase, while I was driving to Alresford for training, my phone rang. I pulled in to answer the call, which was from Mr Malone, asking me to call in and see him before training. This I did, meeting him at our ground, the Denplan. He couldn't look at me while he said, 'I'm relieving you of your position as Manager, as I don't think you are the right man for the job.' I didn't answer him, I just walked out.

'Where are you going?' he asked.

'Training,' I said. 'I've a squad which Neil Hards and I are preparing to win the biggest trophy this club never won, the FA Vase.' With that, I walked out, got in my car and drove to Alresford College to take training which I had planned prior to the Vase final at St Andrews.

The session went well, with a full turnout of players and Neil Hards, my assistant, who didn't realise he was going to lead the club out as manager for the Vase final. At the end of the session, I got everyone together and told them that I was no longer Manager of the club, and that the Chairman had called me into the office at the ground to tell me, quote 'I wasn't the right man for the job.' A bunch of the players and my friend and assistant Neil Hards threatened to quit the club, which I could understand, but here we were, having already won the League, being 15 points clear of everyone. The Wessex League Cup was already ours and we were preparing for the FA Vase final. I turned to Neil and said, 'Take the boys to Birmingham and win the FA Vase, giving us a clean sweep for the League and cups we entered in 2004.'

I shook hands with everyone and said, thank you to the players and Neil for all of their hard work, and excellent football, and I drove home, still not understanding 'I wasn't the right man for the job.'

The boys won the Vase, which completed the treble for the club, although I didn't attend the final. What a great achievement for the season! The fact was, I couldn't understand why I wasn't the right man for the job, until I read my contract some years later. While looking through my collection of football memorabilia, I came across my contract for 2003-2004 as Manager of Winchester City FC. After I had read it, I got to the bonus payments if we had won all three trophies. Only then did I realise why I wasn't the right man for the job: with only the FA Vase to win, my contract payment bonuses added up to a lot of money. I picked up the phone and rang Mr Malone. 'I now know why you sacked me, having read my contract.'

'You are right,' replied Mr Malone, 'I couldn't afford your bonus figure. If you had gone on to win the FA Vase, as our Manager, I could not pay you.'

I answered him, 'Leading the club out for the FA Vase final, and winning it would have been, but never will be, one of the greatest moments of my football career, but you took that away from me, because you would not be able to pay me what you had written into my contract.'

When footballing friends asked me, 'Why?' I had no answer for anyone.

The non-League paper did a front page spread on my achievements, while needing to know why I was sacked after winning the League, the Senior Cup and the FA Vase, but I had nothing to tell them, not knowing at the time about the bonus structure on my contract. To this day, when I bump into some of my players who took part in the success we achieved, and explain to them, I know it's easy to say, but I would have thrown a party for those players and staff, who saw us through that season, but it wasn't to be. If anyone needs to know the truth then ask Mr Malone, but whether he tells you or not, is up to him.

Salisbury FC to AFC Totton

After I left Winchester Football Club, Nick Holmes asked me to join Salisbury Football Club as a coach, but said that if another club came for me as manager he said he would understand if I wanted to join that club as manager.

I was helping as a coach, working alongside Tommy Widdrington, the ex-Saints midfield player, and Barry Blankley, a very good defender, for a period of three months, learning, as well as enjoying my stay at Salisbury FC, when the Chairman of AFC Totton, John Dawson, asked me if I would take the manager's job at his club. Not knowing too much about the club, apart from three or four of their players, I asked if I could come to the club and meet him for a chat. Then I would join the club, or respectfully not. As it was, I agreed to join Totton in February 2003 and we won the League Cup Final, beating Eastleigh at A.F.C. Newbury's ground, with young Paddy James clinching the winner in the dying minutes, and also finishing third in the League. It was a short, yet very successful term, which I enjoyed very much, adding new players, staff and the Chairman, with his Directors, to my list of friends in football.

Bashley FC 2003-04

After my short term at Totton, I took the manager's job at Bashley FC in the Dr Martens League, Eastern Division. Bashley is a small village in the New Forest with a population of 292, having one shop, a petrol station and a very well presented football ground, with a club house, good changing rooms behind the grandstand and a very good training area behind the bottom goal. The club had competed in the Premier Division of the Southern League in the 1990-91 season, finishing a very creditable tenth. In 1997 Ray Pinney took over as chairman, and my good friend Jimmy Case was their manager, having a very successful season, finishing third in the Southern Division, and reaching the semi-final of the League Cup. Since then, they have managed to maintain a good standard, although some of the away games do mean getting the squad together for a coach trip to the likes of Folkestone, Tonbridge, or Dartford on a Tuesday evening. The chairman sorted the travel for away games, no matter where we were playing, and we rarely suffered the lack of a full squad, because of the attitude of the players.

When I talked to Barry Blanley, the previous manager, he was very upbeat about the club in general. The only problem for me was picking up a couple of players en route and making sure that we were on time for both training and home games. As I said earlier, the players were excellent and as the season went on we, Rick Haysom and I, felt that, given the travelling we and the players were doing, both for home and away games, during the 90 minutes our legs were going with 15 minutes left of the 90 minutes, we were conceding goals, which were costing us points. Rick, my assistant, and I both felt we were good, regarding our training, but the travelling, after our players had worked an eight-hour shift, was taking its toll.

Do we cut the training down to an hour? If we have a match on a Tuesday or Wednesday, do we cancel training and ask our players to train on their own, giving them a night off because of travelling? We tried different ideas and the players reacted in a professional manner, however when the weather changed and grounds were heavy, that took its toll, but we finished in the top half of the League, and got to the quarter-final of the Senior Hampshire Cup. The respect should go to our squad of players, who never complained and allowed me to enjoy my stay at Bashley until I left the club half way through the season.

Bashley to Salisbury City

After Bashley, Nick Holmes asked me if I would come back to Salisbury City to take the youth team, which I did. I loved every minute, as some of the youth team squad seemed destined for a good career, which has proved right. Today, they are playing in higher non-League teams; the likes of Joe Fisher, Johnathan Davies, Lewis Benson and Jamie Barron, to name but a few. The job suited me, as they listened and put into practice what was asked, working to improve their skills and fitness, while knowing what was asked when we didn't have the ball.

The following season I took the reserves who had joined the new suburban league, and asked the majority of the youth players to step up. To be honest, most of the players were youth lads, with three or four of the reserves, who were not getting a game with the first eleven. Nick kept a good bench for the first team, while we covered the new league unbeaten and won the Suburban Cup at Imber Court, the Metropolitan Police's stadium, beating Dunstable in the final. Simon Browne worked with me and I'm sure, if you asked either of us, it would be our best achievement. Just ask Arsene Wenger!

AFC Totton

John Dawson and his Directors for Totton AFC were very good
to work with. As Chairman, John Dawson ran everything by the
directors and me, and meetings were arranged so that we were
all allowed to voice our opinions regarding football matters. His
attitude towards the club he ran was exemplary, along with his
directors. So much so, that, although I don't see many of their games,
they have now progressed to a higher level in non-League football,
and I have to congratulate both the staff and players during the
seasons of progress, while feeling the foundations were laid many
seasons ago, by the Chairman and his friends, whose love for the
club and football was plain to see.

I was fortunate to work under their guidance, which left me to get
on with managing the players and staff, to set the standards that
both our players and supporters wanted. Given that we were a
club where supporters could attend Southampton FC and other
non-League matches, the club had a very good following. Like all
supporters who attend games and pay for the privilege, they want
to see their club win and play good football. If they are losing, yet
still trying to work hard under the circumstances, then both players
and those who have paid to see their team go home having had their
money's worth watching an honest game. Yes, we all want the team
we support to win; however, when I played, coached or managed,
the games were more honest then, no play-acting amongst players
who roll about as if they have been poleaxed, then one minute later
are up and running as if nothing has happened. This diving to gain a
free kick, and holding of players on corners and free kicks needs to
be stopped.

I, like most football lovers, have been watching the World Cup games
in Russia, and I had been hoping that referees and linesman, (sorry,
referees' assistants) and VAR will cut out this so-called 'win at all
costs' and bring back honest tackling and honest players, because a
lot of people who watch today's games are losing interest.

Salisbury FC Youth and Reserves 2007-08

While enjoying my work at Salisbury, running the youth and reserve
squads with Simon Browne, the club had entered a team into the

Suburban League, which Nick had asked Simon and me to take. This meant selecting a squad from the youth and reserves who were eligible and good enough to take part in this new league. Actually, the league had formed in 1971, with a northern division and a southern division, which we, Salisbury were in, and a premier division. We started the league in August 2007 and come the end of the season at 7th April, we were unbeaten and remained so, when we competed against Dunstable Town in the Suburban League Cup Final at Imber Court, winning the Cup to cap off an unbeaten run in our first season, of which Simon Browne, the players and I were very proud. The trophies were presented to us at the Suburban League dinner at Sandown Park at the end of the season.

Salisbury City FC 2008-09

Hoping to start pre-season in 2009, Nick Holmes, the manager and a friend, called Barry Blankley, Ian Harris and me into his office. Due to financial problems, we would have to leave the club. We were surprised, as it was to be the three of us. We could see how difficult it was for Nick to tell us the bad news. We looked at each other, then shook hands with Nick and Tommy Widdrington his assistant. No questions were needed, apart from thank-yous for what we had done. With that, we left, all looking for new jobs in football.

Not long after, as the new season was about to get under way, Dave Diaper asked me if I would help him out, due to the new league he was in, by watching the teams they were due to play and asking if I could recommend any players to join him at Sholing FC, which he was managing at the time. To date, he is the chairman at Sholing, a good team and club, very strong and always in the top three or four in the Wessex League. I put this down to Mr Dave Diaper, a gentleman who loves his club and football. Well done Dave!

Alton Town FC

In the 2011-12 season, I was asked to return to manage Alton Town and yes, I took the job. But after helping at Sholing, with no pressure and realising I was getting older, I realised, while my love of football was still there, the need to manage a club and be successful was taking its toll. While helping Sholing for Dave Diaper and carrying the pressure for results of the club, I found it enjoyable, without too much personal pressure. But at Alton, I found the driving to the likes of Hungerford and back on a Saturday and away games on a Tuesday evening to coach was the only downside. Given that I had enjoyed the 90 minutes and taking the information back to Dave, which helped, I decided to resign from Alton Town. I explained to Mr McKell that while I enjoyed football, being a manager was taking up most of the week with training and games, which I wasn't enjoying as much as I used to. He understood and I stayed until he found a new manager, then I left on good terms.

Fleet Town FC
Not long after resigning from Alton Town, my friend and football manager of Fleet Town FC, Craig Davies, asked me if I could help out with some coaching and training, which, as a friend, I did. If I were to pick people in football who needed a helping hand to turning things around, when the club they were managing was not responding to what was required, then Craig is man enough to ask for help, even if it's just a change of face taking coaching, or the shape of the team.

I thoroughly enjoyed helping out, as it kept me involved. After being at Fleet Town for about four weeks, helping Craig as a friend, I attended some of the games, hoping to see any improvement. Not that it was about what I had done, but what Craig deserved, being a good manager of players and with his knowledge of football. As they say, he has been there and done it. Craig has four players in his squad who I'm sure will be in his starting line-up and be an asset to his squad. Once the season had started, I would be down to the Denplan ground, watching and enjoying the football.

Scouting for Richard Hill, Manager of Eastleigh
Richard Hill, the Manager of Eastleigh FC was looking for a couple of scouts to cover the teams and individual players in the top standard of non-League football. The two he asked were Guy Butters and me. Guy was an ex-Tottenham Hotspur defender and a great lad to know. We used to stay in touch, regarding the teams we had to watch and any players who stood out among the ones we had gone to watch. Richard was more interested in the opposition: the system they played, whether they were home or away and any free kicks, so I made sure I took notes regarding both teams.

On Friday evening, after Richard had told us who we were watching, it was either my turn to phone Guy or his to tell me where he was covering. When he told me he was travelling to Eastbourne, I said, 'You can't be, as Richard has asked me to cover Eastbourne's game.'

After talking for five minutes about whether one of us should speak to him, we both decided I would watch both teams and Guy would cover free kicks and set pieces, by drawing them on A4 paper. This is just what we did. When we put our reports in on the Tuesday, prior to training, Richard asked 'Why did you both go to the same game?'

'Because you asked me to go to the Eastbourne game', I said and Guy said, 'You asked me to go to the Eastbourne game, boss.'

'Don't you talk to each other when you know where you are both going?' 'No', we both said.

What actually happened was we arrived, we asked each other, 'What are we doing at the same game?'

We went into the bar after sitting together, watching the game and agreeing I would take the two teams and Guy would cover set pieces. After the game, we both went into the bar until the supporters in cars had cleared the car park, when in came Tommy Widdrington, who we both knew. He came over to our table and asked us, 'What are you both doing here?'

'Well, it's not a long story Tommy, but it was a mix-up on Richard Hill's part, so here we are.'

After 20 minutes or so, we said our cheerios and Tommy walked out to the car park with us, asking, 'Where is your car, Robbo? Mmm, I get it, Richard is a good friend of mine. I must phone him,' he said, then waved us off. We hoped he didn't.

On Tuesday we both drove to Fleet in Hampshire to collect our expenses and gave Richard our reports, which he didn't even look at, as we were playing in the Hampshire Senior Cup. He then took our expenses from his inside coat pocket to give us. As soon as the final whistle went, we both decided to leave, saying our well-dones to the team.

No, Tommy Widdrington didn't say anything, we said nothing and, to our surprise, Richard didn't ask any questions either. Maybe it wasn't a mistake, asking his two scouts to cover the same game.My hope is that those who read this short story don't bump into Richard after reading it. We are both very sorry Richard.

Petersfield FC 2017

While having a few days break at our friends, Steve and Wendy Conway, who live in Coalville, just outside Leicester, my phone rang. I answered the call, asking, 'Who is it please?' 'Gary Lines', was the answer. 'Yes Gary, what can I do for you?' I asked. 'We would like you to join Petersfield FC as Manager.'

'Well, I'm in Leicester at the moment and will be back on 14th October. If that is OK Gary, I could come up to Petersfield FC for a chat with you and your Chairman?' 'Yes, that is fine, I will speak to the Chairman.' 'OK, thanks, see you then.'

I drove up to the club on 15th October and met Gary Lines, Director of Football at Petersfield and we discussed the amount I wanted weekly to manage the first team. I said '£50 per week would cover my expenses; that would be fine.' I asked if that would be OK with the Chairman. 'No problem,' he said, 'I'll deal with this appointment regarding Petersfield.'

We had our photographs taken, shaking hands on the deal and the photograph and appointment were reported in the local papers the following day.

We had quite a good start, with a win and a draw in our first couple of games. Given our training nights down at Park Community School in Leigh Park estate only had half of a pitch to carry out our training sessions, things looked OK. There were often late arrivals, which was awkward. Although I was allowing for work and traffic, we rarely had all of the first team squad there on time to start. After a few sessions, I realised something wasn't right behind the scenes. While I was getting to know the players, I decided to take them to one side.

'Wait until the end of the month and you will realise what is the reason, Robbo,' they said.

I soon knew what the players were on about at the end of my

first month. Stuart Green was working with me at an apartment in Havant. We were carrying out alterations to a bathroom for a disabled lady I knew and, during our break for lunch, Stuart told me all he knew about the club, regarding the first team squad. Fancy having to admit and accept that the first team squad were heading for relegation and there was nothing I could do about it.

Ian Saunders had done a very good job getting promotion on two occasions, then left the club, so I phoned Ian for a chat regarding Petersfield.

Ian was very honest with me, but was very surprised when I told him of my problems. I had no intention of walking out on my players, so I phoned the Chairman, asking if he could meet me for a chat regarding my problems. We met a few days later at the McDonalds in Bedhampton and I asked him for an answer about what I had heard. There was no denial from him, apart from asking me to get a team of ex-professionals to play Petersfield at the end of the season. This would allow him to be able to pay me from the takings.

I thought for a minute or two, but realised this was something I could not do under any circumstances and I am still waiting.

However, I would like to say my thank you to all of my players and staff, who may have missed the odd training session and been late turning up for the odd match and sometimes had to play out of position. Thank you and a big thank you to Big Matt, who worked with me through all of the problems and one Saturday morning signed before 11am to play in goal for us to play Kempston Rovers away.

You were fantastic, Matt, and everyone in the ground that day agreed. I wished we had ten others like you mate, we would have been at the other end of the League.

But alas, it wasn't to be. However, for me there was a massive plus; I had made a new friend for life.

FOOTBALL - MY VIEWS ON THE GAME TODAY

World Cup 2018

Today, 24th June 2018, is a big day for all of us who love our football and love our country. England is live on BBC against Panama.

We should be too good for them, but as we all know, there are no certainties in football. I just hope the referee and his three helpers are strong enough, when controlling the game. VAR is there to help if needed, yet it has been proved to be a game changer in some games, especially when it is obvious, yet not given. Come on England!

I wonder if, during training, some coaches and managers encourage these trips, when running; the pulling of shirts when a player has gone past you, with or without the ball; the holding of players in the 18-yard box from corners and free kicks. When I played, the ball was inside the area from a corner. Why allow it on the outside edge? These so-called allowances are spoiling games. I imagine Jack Taylor and Pierluigi Collina would make their feelings known to players, prior to the kick-off, and they would help to stamp out all that I have mentioned and more, bringing our game back to what it used to be.

What a great result for England, 6-1 against Panama, and didn't we play well for 80 minutes? But the best thing for me was the finishing, something we are not always good at. Yes, Harry Kane is a gem, his penalties were first class and his third goal, well, how lucky! But it counts. However, Jesse Lingard's was top of the list for me. With Belgium coming up on Thursday, that is going to be a game we should be looking to win. Fingers crossed. I felt that the referee played a big part in the result, whereas previous officials, including assistant referees, have allowed blatant shirt pulling and wrestling players to the ground to go unpunished.

Regarding the England team, I feel that our full-backs, Trippier, Young and Walker, have played well, both going forward and defensively, although I do prefer Rose at left-back. Our keeper, Pickford, hasn't really been tested yet, but I feel at times when we keep the ball at the back, he allows the opposition to get too near to him when he has the ball at his feet. Come on England! Bring the Cup home where it belongs, the true home of football.

Tuesday 3rd July, England versus Colombia tonight. I will say, before we talk about the game tonight, that I have been surprised by the amount of supporters who have travelled to Russia from far and wide to follow their country, and also pleased by the way that Russia have, so far, welcomed all-comers, without any trouble. I do expect, now that we are in the knockout stage, that those teams expected to go through are finding their opposition very well organised at the back, then catching their opponents on the break. When you lose to the likes of Spain, Germany and Argentina before the quarter-final, you realise there are no guarantees to progress, just because you are expected to win.

I felt it was about time Belgium stepped up to the mark, given the players they have. Watching them last night go two down to Japan, I did wonder if they could come back and win the game, but when they did attack Japan in numbers, Japan looked awful defensively and Belgium took advantage of that, finishing off with a winner just before the final whistle. I've often wondered why Belgium haven't won the Euros with the squad they have. Maybe the World Cup is what they are after. They certainly could go close.

Back to England's game tonight. At this level every player should be ready to give their best, which I'm sure they are, but are they good enough to be part of the squad? Yes, I'm happy with Gareth Southgate as Manager, but is he going to select his best players in their preferred positions? First of all, Jordan Pickford in goal. I should be jumping for joy with him, being a Sunderland lad as he is, but he worries me when he has to play football at the back. As a shot stopper, he is good, but this is the World Cup.

Danny Rose, Tottenham and England left-back is, in my opinion, our best left-back. At right-back I'm undecided between Young and Kyle Walker; both are good enough. I want Harry Maguire as one of the centre-backs. I will say that I am not a fan of Dier in the midfield as a holding player and Sterling up top with Harry Kane does not fill me with confidence. Kane is a must, but I would play Lingard just off Kane. Still, what do I know?

Well, we all have our own feelings on who Gareth will pick and while I am not a fan of Dele Alli, maybe he could play just off Harry Kane, with Lingard as an attacking midfielder. Come on England! If we do beat Colombia tonight and prefer other players in the team when we play in the quarter-final, then I will be fine and keep my changes to see us through to the final. But are we good enough? Why not?

It's now 10.20 pm and, after watching the game, I thought Colombia were a disgrace with their antics. Still, they took the game to extra time and then to a penalty shoot-out, which as you all know, for a change, we won, with Dier scoring the winner. Mind you, I hope you agree, that Sterling and Dele Alli contributed very little up top, while Dier's first few passes went to a Colombian player and, as extra time went on, we looked second best. As for the referee, he could have stopped their antics during the first half by looking at the VAR and producing a red card, instead of the five yellows during the first 90 minutes.

The match verses Colombia finished some time ago and I've managed to calm down, as we won on the penalty shoot-out. During the 90 minutes, I was furious, as I'm sure most of you watching also were. Can we progress to the semis? Not if we don't finish teams off in the 90 minutes, as we didn't look fit enough during extra time. As I'm English and a footballer, of course I want us to win, but I keep questioning myself, are we good enough? I'm not sure.

The World Cup has allowed me to add these pages in this book I am in the process of writing, and enjoying, apart from tonight's game against Colombia. Watching them angered me so much, because if the game we invented has turned into what I watched, it is not the football I played. Let's not get carried away by elbowing, wrestling in the box and surrounding the referee. Tonight's game, which Colombia brought to the Word Cup, was disgraceful.

Let us have a look so far, as we are now into the quarter-final stage. The hosts, Russia, have done an excellent job. Yes, there is a lot of distance between the cities and stadia, both for teams and supporters. As yet, there have been very few problems between supporters prior to games and after, according to the BBC, ITV and Sky.

We are approaching the competition games, where players, coaches and managers must get it right regarding selection and the system to play, based on the opposition and fitness of players who have suffered injuries. We will all have our favourite players for each position in the team and rightly so. Add that to the work rate when we don't have the ball and that shows us who really wants it. I must say well done to a player in the squad, who I don't rate as having the quality to play for England, but who put the penalty away under immense pressure, to take us to the next level. Well done Eric Dier, you showed quality.

With regard to discipline from players, those who roll about as if they have been shot by a sniper, the wrestling from corners in the 18-yard box and free-kicks, etc., I would hope that FIFA, the FA and other governing bodies would allow referees to use the sin bin for a period of 15 minutes for players who commit these fouls, with no allowance to bring on players during this time and for the fourth official, as he is in touch with the referee, to keep the time when the 15 minutes is up, given that the referee will allow the guilty player back on when the ball is out of play.

I realise we should not resort to these kinds of rules, but if it were to stop this acting, which has no place in the game of football, then we could enjoy the game within the rules. For those who have been a lover of our wonderful game, cast your mind back and tell us all when you last saw these antics, when you shouted at the officials for allowing players to stay on the pitch. These blatant fouls, to gain advantage over your team, whether it is in the World Cup, the Euros, the Champions' League, La Liga or any game you are watching. It's not football!

Let us look at the excuses we could give for this kind of taking advantage outside of the laws of the game. There are no excuses. No matter what level you have chosen to watch, if there are officials and the rules are accepted, whether you agree or disagree, surely you want your team to win within the rules, to win because they were the best team on the day, in your opinion? Or are you a supporter who goes home and tells your mates, or your family, who are watching Match of the Day, 'Oh, see our centre-half take their player out of the game with an elbow across the head! Or wrestle him to the ground.'

If that is what you go to football for, you have no place to be there. I'm sure we all, who love football, love to play for a team, not just to go out there and kick the player we are marking. Does that make you feel good? If it does, then why don't you take up boxing? Or does that allow the guy you have just hit to hit you back? Yes, it does and you don't like that. Football definitely does need more discipline, but we play and watch to show skill, whether you have the ball at your feet, or you are looking for that pass to your team mate, giving him that chance to score, or covering a team mate and telling him you are covering him, allowing him to make a challenge for the ball. Reading the game, whether with or without the ball, will give you a chance to move to a better standard, whereas kicking and bullying your opponents will eventually give your mates and manager the reason to tell you are not doing your team mates any favours, giving away free kicks around your 18-yard box or committing fouls in your opponents' 18-yard box from a corner or free kick.

We saw two sides of Colombia. In the first half they gave the referee lots of do, surrounding him, a ploy that can give officials a problem, seeing who committed the offence, then blaming our players. Yet in the second half, at times they played some good stuff. Anyway, they got what they deserved.

Well done England! England 2, Sweden 0 and a very good performance to boot!

I will stick to the performance regarding Raheem Sterling. He should be told to release the ball in the 18-yard area, when he has the chance to lay it off to a team mate. Yes, the long-term professionals on the panels, after games we have won, say his pace, etc. puts defences under pressure, but what if we didn't win? Yes, a draw gives us a point, but we are now in the semis. It's a team game.

Credit to the England squad and credit to Eric Dier, who stepped up under immense pressure, in having to take the penalty. I still feel, if he does start for us in the semis against Croatia, then he needs to keep an eye on Modric, their captain, as most things go through him when they have the ball. I also feel that Harry Kane wasn't too involved in the quarter-final, as I'm sure he would admit, but maybe he will come alive and find the goals for our win to the final. Now that would be just what we, and Harry Kane, would want! 'It's coming home!'

I must say a thank you to Gareth Southgate and the FA who chose Gareth to manage England, after Big Sam. I do think we all felt after the first few games that Sam was a very good choice. However, after him stepping down and the FA having to find a replacement, I feel that Gareth is quietly managing his squad and we do seem to be getting better with every game. Let's hope that one more win, against Croatia, will prove that young players don't seem to carry the same pressure as those who are expected to play well and that is a good lesson to managers who continue to play experienced players, when a good mix of experience and quality young players seems to be the answer. Let's hope so anyway.

The last few games to decide the final two, and the third and fourth places, did not impress me at all.

I felt that if our work rate and desire were there, that would give us third place against Belgium. Yet, we were found wanting on ability, as we were against Croatia, which disappointed me, given the talk about Harry Kane, Stirling and Lingard. At the back, the defenders did their job with the goalkeeper, and not only did their job at the back, but contributed in set pieces to our goal tally, which was more than was asked.

I thought that Young, Maguire, Stones and Trippier, along with Pickford in goal, showed me the desire which is needed to convince the supporters, whether they played or just watched football, that their team gave the impression that, yes, we will win this game. But I am afraid I never felt that at all, either in the semis or third place play-off. Well done Pickford, Trippier and Maguire, at seven out of ten!

To sum up the Word Cup competition in Russia, based on the stories prior to the start, I felt that, as a supporter, the competition would be so difficult to beat, both on and off the pitch. Well done Russia! Apart from one tiny problem, I'm sure that, after all is settled, the Russian Football Association will applaud themselves whe watching the recordings of the games.

Could we have done better? We will have to see who is still around in 2022 in Qatar. I'm sure Gareth Southgate will be, but he needs a captain who isn't afraid to get hold of team mates verbally and make sure they raise their game, both with the ball and without it. Whoever says teams don't need an experienced player, usually in midfield or at the back, wearing the captain's armband, is kidding himself. Take the armband and pressure off Kane, allowing him to play, and give it to someone who takes in every minute of the game, while managing his team on the pitch.

My Two Sons

Darren, who at present is 49 years old, had a very interesting and successful football career, but the main success we, his mum and dad, wanted was for Darren to do well regarding his schooling. He loved his football, from day one, while still working hard at his education, but I believe if you are born from a family of sporting parents, you could inherit some of their ability. The good news was, regarding a job after school, Darren became a Civil Servant and, to date, is working within the Royal Navy and can look back on a very successful working career, while remembering and enjoying the football he played as a midfield play maker. Throughout his various clubs he was classed as a free kick and penalty taker. Darren played for me at two clubs, yet as I travel around watching clubs, those who speak very highly of his ability and attitude are managers and players, who he played for and with. They always ask after him, which, as a father, allows pride in me, while listening to their praise.

Scott, my younger son, played most of his football on a Sunday morning, during his younger years, which allowed me to watch him as a 13-year-old, until he was 16 and the Manager, Mr Thomson, knew his stuff. Scott was a natural goal scorer and, as he progressed, he never lost the knack of being in the right place at the right time, finishing off the moves for his team. Mr Thomson was the Manager of Unicorn and, as time went on, he would say to me, 'Scott needs a much better standard to enable him to better himself.'

I knew he was fit enough at the age of 16 for Sunday football, but would he be strong enough against the centre-halves in non-League at a good level? Well, the only way was to give him a go. I took him to Worthing FC, who I managed in the early 90s, and sat him on the bench, thinking I could bring him on in the last ten or 15 minutes, hoping his fresh legs would allow him chances, which even in the Diadora League I felt he would cope with well. I was right, he did.

Watching the game for 80 minutes, then having ten minutes to show his ability, was his learning curve, regarding his football and experience, at quite a high level. From Sunday football, maybe it was too high, but I still felt he would do well, given time. However, I did realise our forwards were very good and no way could I start him. But after a short while, he didn't feel ten or 15 minutes on the pitch was enough, as he was giving his Saturday and a mid-week game to watch.

Darren, his brother, was the first team centre-midfield general, setting forwards off with chances and taking all set pieces for us. Yet, to this day, I know if he had stayed in football, he would have made it at a very good non-League level, then who knows from there?

Both Darren and Scott have very good jobs and families. My grandson, Adam, is also a very good player, but doesn't have the ambition to get involved. Scott had two lovely daughters and I sometimes go to watch Scott, Ella's boyfriend, play. Scott is a very good athlete. I feel he could be outstanding at 400 metres. Still, what do I know?

My Daughter Lisa

Lisa, my daughter, has given my wife, Ann, and me two lovely grandsons, but they do not have any interest in football. They are both very good at school, as the reports show, but neither Joseph nor Oliver shows any interest regarding sport. I have tried to get them involved, but once again, school-work takes priority, which I do respect. Yet my daughter Lisa was an athlete, sprinting and hurdling for Hampshire and going abroad to France to compete.

Things were certainly looking up, until Lisa represented Hampshire at Portsmouth in a county championship. She had completed her track runs and then was asked to compete in the long jump, to gain points for the team, as they had no one to do the long jump. Lisa agreed, saying she was a track athlete and had never done the long jump. After Lisa had finished her track events, we walked over to the long jump area. On her first and only jump, she landed awkwardly in the sand and had to be helped to her feet. She said her lower back hurt and she found it very difficult to walk. In the end, we took her to the hospital, as the pain in her lower back worsened. To this day, Lisa walks with a constant limp. After treatment and advice from doctors, we realised Lisa's long jump for her club was a jump too far. What seemed to be a promising career in athletics came to an abrupt end. Bad luck darling!

My Niece and Nephew - Amber and Zach

I feel it is important to write about the importance of giving your best to something you wish to achieve as you get older. We all had dreams when we were growing up and I am lucky that a brother and sister in my family, from County Durham, have excelled in their aim to succeed.

Three years ago, my niece decided to attend Southampton University to study sports media, mainly football, and came away with an honours degree. Also, to cap off her success, she was picked to travel to Russia and, through work, give her opinion in words on the World Cup. I attended her presentation at the Civic Hall in Southampton, along with my wife, Ann, my sister Rosalind and her mam and dad, Jayne and Ian. Well done Amber Hemming, we are all very proud of you and your achievement.

How unusual is it for two young people to achieve their dreams, especially a brother and sister? I'm sure some of you reading this will be saying, yes, I know friends whose children have fulfilled their dreams. Well, I know people whose aim has been achieved, but only through hard work and total commitment. Our Amber's brother, Zach Hemming, had dreams of being a goalkeeper. When he was invited to join Newcastle United at the age of ten, that was the start. Two weeks ago, on his eighteenth birthday, after joining Middlesbrough FC and spending the last seven seasons with them, he signed his full-time contract. My brother-in-law, John, has played a big part in taking him to training and games during his apprenticeship in the academy. His dream has come to reality. Well done Zach! I have watched him, both at Brighton and at games when I have been seeing the family up north. I wish both Amber and Zach a good working life, after fulfilling their dreams through hard work. When you have a talent and you work at it, your dreams can be fulfilled.

Possible Retirement from Management

Leaving Petersfield Town at the end of the 2017-18 season was something I didn't enjoy. Football, apart from my family and the journeys it had taken me on, when I was in Her Majesty's Service, had covered amazing games, amazing players and grounds abroad and at home, which some players would love to have on their CV.

Yes, when you are a player, playing alongside good team mates and under a good manager, you may lose some games and maybe grab a point away from home, but as long as you play as a team and do your clever tricks as a forward, in and around the opponents' 18-yard box, then help out when you are under pressure, in and around your half, you will be recognised as a player who puts in a shift for his team, win, lose or draw. You will be selected for your next game and respected within your squad when you put the club shirt on for the team, after training and coaching in preparation. Do your tricks as an attacker in the right areas and as a defender show your strength and your mobility when tackling, or covering a team mate.

As a player in the midfield, you could be picked for creating the chances for your forwards, or a holding player, in front of a back three or four, while your work rate for the team is essential and will be noticed by your mates, the manager and those watching.

As a defender, you will be asked to go wide, whether right or left back, and midfield players will find you and allow you the ball, while giving you support and drawing an opposition player out to cover you, allowing forwards to use the areas when the cross is delivered.

Being a centre-forward, you are almost expected to score when a chance arrives and your connection on the ball has to be good and finish in the net.

Now regarding the goalkeeper, who is there to stop you from scoring, unless you have played in goal on a regular week in, week out, without being asked to step down, other than because of an injury, then I would not offer my coaching to a goalkeeper, apart from training with the ball at his feet and passing to a team mate, with the accuracy of an outfield player. This is now part of a goalkeeper's ability in the modern game.

Coaching the Modern Way

Please don't think I know it all, regarding football, but when you are working under Alan Mullery, Gerry Armstrong and Peter Osgood, if you don't listen and learn and bring some of their knowledge into your coaching and training, then you haven't learnt anything. I agree that, professionally, they have daily training, and some clubs in top-flight football have coaches who cover every position in the first team squad, whereas in non-League football, clubs cannot afford this, but that would be the only problem.

Football is the same when coached individually or collectively. It's up to non-League players to listen, then adapt what is being asked of them. The one thing with non-League players is that you can blame team mates if you feel things are not working, but in the professional game, you find, after a while, you are wearing the sub's shirt on the bench, then when the transfer windows arrive, you are either loaned-out, or moved on to another club in a lower League. So it's up to you as a player to avoid this, by listening and working hard.

Football – Has it Changed for the Better or Worse?

I started playing as far back as my sixth birthday on the big field in the village of Oakenshaw, County Durham, way back in 1953, when my mam and dad bought me a small leather football. This was because of the two local non-League teams, Willington AFC, who played Bishop Auckland AFC in the Amateur Cup Final at Wembley in 1950. It was Willington's first final at Wembley and as the town was only two miles away, we supported Willington. Mind you, Bishop Auckland was only six or seven miles away, but for my dad and me, at the time, Willington didn't stand a chance again the mighty Bishop Auckland. Bishop's honours list read; FA Amateur Cup winners seven times, Durham County Cup winners four times, Northern League champions ten times, appeared in the final eleven times.

Could any team beat Bishop's amateur internationals? Well, an estimated crowd of 70,000 went to watch at Wembley and saw my team Willington win 4-0. As I grew older, the result became more important to me, even though the Bishops were back at Wembley playing Crook Town in the final. Crook Town was about three miles from my village, yet once again a big crowd turned up at Wembley for the 2-2 draw and the replay at Newcastle United finished with another draw. The following replay was at Middlesbrough, where Crook Town lifted the cup after a 1-0 win.

Nowadays, the game would have been finished after extra time, with a penalty shoot-out, which I think is a good way to finish when you have the winners and the losers. The first replay in those days was costly to the supporters and a second replay even more so. So, I do think penalty shoot-outs are the answer after extra time. Also, the supporters see their team lift the trophy.

Let's look back to football in the 1950s. I was very lucky, in a way, that the miners' holiday was always in July. We always went to Blackpool, sometimes for two weeks, depending on the finances. My dad knew I was going to ask him to take me to watch Blackpool during their pre-season training, especially if they had a game in the evening. Yes, in those days things were different. The ball was leather and sewn together, so when it was wet, it was very heavy and the 60-yard passes you see today, you rarely saw in those days, unless it was a big strong centre-half or full-back hoofing it clear of his 18-yard box.

The boots had studs, or bars, so players could grip the turf. Mind you, during the games they played in the 50s, if it had rained the night before, then after 20 minutes you had 22 players and a referee running around on a ploughed field, trying to use the ball and time their tackles so as not to give a free kick away. In those days you had wingers hugging the line, ready to attack the full-backs and hoping to get a good cross in for their big strong centre-forward to head the ball into the net.

I remember in those days, either watching Sunderland at Roker Park, or Blackpool at Bloomfield Road. There were names that your grandfather would know, who even in these conditions, showed skill on the ball, either crossing as a winger, heading for goal or tackling as a defender. When you talk about professional footballers in those days and in those conditions, you realised just how good they were. Blackpool in the 50s had a very good side, but not a squad. The squad was the reserve side, not forgetting you didn't have four or five subs waiting to replace injured players. Also, you did have an outfield player who could replace your goalkeeper if he had to come off due to an injury.

Ask your grandfather, or your mate's grandfather, about football and players in those days. Better still, go to your library and take out the autobiography of Stanley Matthews of Stoke FC, then Blackpool FC and England, Footballer of the Year in 1948 (the first ever); European Footballer of the Year in 1956. He was also the first footballer to be awarded the CBE and, following that, the first footballer to be knighted, in 1965. He remains, to this day, the only one to receive the award, while still playing. He was the Football Writers' Player of the Year in 1948 and 1963. Not a bad collection of awards, and not awarded to anyone else to this day.

That is how good Stanley Matthews was. In 1999, I was invited to London to honour the careers of the football greats and Sir Stanley Matthews was being recognised as one of them. I did have the pleasure of shaking his hand and now realise what an honour it was for me, having read his book *The Way it Was* and finding that he played his last game at the age of 70 in Brazil, having competed in over 697 games.

How much has changed in football? The kit, the boots, the grounds, the surfaces, the balls and the rules. I wonder how good Sir Stanley would be today, given these changes. For the better, I'm sure. But Sir Stanley passed away on 23rd February 2000, leaving a legacy which may never be equalled.

I wonder if they have matches in heaven? Yes, the majority of players will be old, however there will be some younger players, like George Best, and I bet when George bumps into Sir Stanley, I can imagine Sir Stanley will be the first to say, 'You were some player George,' while George will be looking over his shoulder at some blonde, saying, 'You were not bad yourself, what's your name again?'

That's life or should I say after-life? Wouldn't that be nice? I bet football will change up above the clouds, playing under floodlights every game, and imagine being an ex-Southampton player, playing for the Saints? They would have to play with a halo on their head and Tottenham ex-players would have to wear bright red spurs on the back of their boots; heaven permitting (not forbid) Wolves would have big teeth and would be allowed to wander around the pitch aimlessly. Heaven forbid what the Arsenal would wear, or not, as the case may be. Just adding a bit of fun to the hopeful after-life, given the names of some of the clubs you support and what they would wear for 90 minutes in heaven!

In my opinion, football at all levels has changed. This, because of the wages that players are on, stops the clubs in the lower leagues going into the transfer market, as the player they want is on wages they cannot pay, which means they now look into the higher levels of non-League teams for a cheaper player. My thanks go to Jamie Vardy of Leicester and England, for setting up his scouting mission, to find players who they feel could step up and fill a position in the professional game, as Jamie did. So far, it has been quite successful. Well done Jamie Vardy!

As I said earlier in the book, I felt that Dave Leworthy was too good to play non-League football, so I took Dave, his dad and his brother up to Tottenham for a trial in a pre-season friendly, and after 45 minutes and three goals, Dave was given a three-year contract. A player who was at Andover with John Waugh, the Manager and myself as player-coach, was Jeremy Stagg, who had been released by Southampton. Jeremy was a right-winger, and after playing alongside him at centre-forward, I knew he was always able to beat his full-back and get a good cross in. He also had the ability and fitness to do work when we didn't have the ball. He kept himself fit and never complained. On Saturday 16th January 1988, I spoke to the newspaper about Jeremy being the best player I had seen and had the pleasure to play with in non-League football.

Yes, football has changed. The training is planned and carried out to get the best out of individuals, then collectively going forward with the ball and finding areas and players to stretch the opposition, making space to punish teams, in or outside their 18-yard box. Also, set piece moves are practised at the end of each session. If you go back to the 1950s, you didn't have full-backs who went past their own wingers. On corners and free kicks from wide areas, you had two or three players who could cross a dead ball into the opposition's 18-yard box, and centre-forwards and centre-halves who were good in the air, hoping the other team didn't get to the ball before they did, directing the ball towards the goal. Now in the 2017-18 season, players bend their free kicks around the wall or over and sometimes under the wall. Set pieces are planned to suit either side of the ball into the area. The equipment today allows that.

In the 1950s and 60s the ball didn't swerve, the boots were heavy leather and the weather played its part on the working of the ball. If it had rained heavily prior to kick-off, the only thing you changed at half time was your shirt and shorts. Yes, football has changed, so much so that the entertainment within teams is shown and the supporters, most times, get value for the money they spend, watching the team they support.

One good thing the FA and governing bodies in all parts of the world brought into football was the back pass to a team's goalkeeper, when he was allowed to pick the ball up and, for a few minutes, kill the game. Now, as we all know, the keeper has to be able to play football, the same as his outfield team mates. A good new rule. The man between the sticks has to be comfortable on the ball in these circumstances. My nephew, a contract goalkeeper with Middlesbrough, practises this until the club is satisfied with the ball at his feet and how he uses it.

Officials During the Game

Let's look at referees, assistant referees, or linesmen, as we older, retired players, managers and the supporters still call them. Would you like to do the job, at any level? Let us show you what a working referee and his assistants go through in a day at non-League level.

It's a Tuesday evening game. Kick-off is 7.45 pm and his game is ten to fifteen miles from his home. He finishes work at 5.30 pm and, let us say, his work place is two or three miles from his home. The traffic isn't too bad, so he is home in ten minutes. The wife, or his mother, has his meal ready and he comfortably finishes his dinner and his cup of tea by 6.15 pm. He then goes to his room for a shower and a change, making sure his gear for the game has been washed and ironed and is ready to pack into his holdall, including his boots, note-book, pencil and whistle.

He then says his cheerios and goes out to drive to the game. He planned his journey, so he can arrive, get ready and have his normal chat with his assistants, then walk out onto the pitch, checking the ball and that the two goalkeepers' kit doesn't clash with the players'. Then it's inline for the respect hand shake between the players and officials. It's now 7.45 pm, kick-off time.

Now I base this on my invitation from the officials to talk about the 90 plus minutes, from a player's point of view and a manager's or coach's.

Every game will throw up some difficult decisions for the referee to make, not forgetting there are possibly 2-3,000 onlookers behind the barriers, telling him his decision was awful, while other are applauding, as they feel he had given the correct decision. So, I ask you – does the game need them? Most definitely! Are the yellow and red cards good for the game? Most definitely! Does the referee need his assistants? Most definitely! Does he need the negative, sometimes obscene remarks he gets from the crowd? Definitely not! Or are they just part and parcel of today's supporters?, not forgetting today's non-League football. Yes, they are. Now, if you are a professional official, I'm sure you would be able to put up with the players, supporters, etc. as the wages in the top end of the game are worth it, just having referees and assisting at games as your main job. So, you people out there who are dreaming of climbing the ladder to the big time, then I commend and thank you all and wish you lovers of football all the best.

Up North to See Family - Tournament at South Shields
South Shields is a non-League club in the north east, called The Mariners. It is a club that, in the last three seasons, has won promotion for the third time in a row, along with numerous other achievements, one being the FA Vase at Wembley. The club is starting the 2018-19 season in the Evostik Premier League on 18th August and I'm sure is looking to gain promotion again and maybe do well in the FA Trophy.

The weekend just gone, I was invited by my best mate Terry to come up for an international trophy tournament, hosted by South Shields Chairman, Geoff Thompson, who has single-handedly changed the fortunes of the club, its players and supporters, and has not finished.

The first match, on Friday 27th July, was between Celtic and the Marseilles under-23s from France. The pitch at Shields was perfect, as they kicked off at 7.30 pm, and the crowd were treated to a very good game, with Marseilles having the edge on Celtic, until there were only ten minutes left. Then the heavens opened, giving the players thunder, lightning and torrential rain, so the referee abandoned the game with the result standing at 1-0 to Marseilles. This had obviously been agreed by both clubs prior to the game starting, but to be honest, the French team were much better than Celtic on the day. The goal was well taken after a very good move from the back four, through to the wide players and finished off, leaving Celtic 1-0 down.

Terry, I, Barry, Nathan, his grandson and Freddie Relf left the ground and, going back to the car, we all hoped for a good day on Saturday 28th, as Shields' under-23s were playing Southampton under-23s at 3 pm kick-off. I was explaining to the lads that the academy at Southampton had been rated by the FA as the most successful academy in English clubs, so I felt that Southampton were favourites to win the tournament.

Saturday 28th and the weather was fine and dry, for a game which I looked forward to. The pitch was perfect for football and we decided to get there before kick-off. We sat in the bar, discussing the game and having a drink, Nathan and me having a soft drink. The chat got round to talking about the progress South Shields had made, and the boys all said it was down to Geoff Thompson, the Chairman, who had backed the club financially, both on and off the pitch, over the past four seasons. I have noticed the ground changes, including cover for the supporters, with only one side to do, which is in progress. The facilities inside include an updated clubhouse, where you can now have meals in a restaurant. Also, outside they have a large tented bar, with tables and chairs. The playing surface is excellent, with a sprinkler system fitted. Along one end of the pitch, Geoff Thompson has taken down a factory and replaced it with a 3G training area for the club, which can be hired when not used by the club. Geoff Thompson deserves success.

South Shields v Southampton was a good game. Both teams used the ball well, but it wasn't long before Southampton had Shields on the back foot. Shields' defence was being opened up, and although their goalkeeper made some very good saves, Southampton was stretching the back four, and it became inevitable that they found the back of the net, showing why they are young professionals. Saying that, South Shields showed their supporters how much they wanted to stay in the game, showing some good players at under-23 level. However, Southampton ran out winners at the end.

On Sunday there was the final, after the third-place play-off at 1 pm between Shields and Celtic, with victory going to Celtic. Shields had done themselves proud and the final between Southampton and Marseilles at 5 pm kick-off was a very good game, with both sides playing some very good football. As it happened, Southampton had the edge when it came to finishing, but what a great weekend, with the supporters enjoying the quality football and watching the trophies being presented. I'm so pleased Terry got tickets for all games and while I still support Sunderland, I also follow Shields in the non-League paper.

As we walked to the car park, I listened to Terry, Barry, Freddie, Nathan and his dad, Neil. Shields, you are in good hands!

Programmes and Books

When I was a young lad, playing my football, I was given some advice from our coach, who said to us, 'You may all progress in football and to different levels, and if the teams you end up playing for produce a programme, then put the programmes, both home and away, in your bag. Then, whatever League, Cup games and standard you achieve, put that programme in your bag, for when you are too old to play, whether it's non-League or League football. Take them home and treasure them, as your football career it is important, especially if you have a son or daughter who follows in your footsteps. You can show them what you achieved and where you played, who you played with and the grounds and Leagues you played in.'

I mentioned daughters earlier and I have had the pleasure of watching my niece play for a women's team on the TV, being very impressed at their ability and the team play they produce. I bet they all take the programmes home and keep a scrapbook. Yes, it is a different level, but take the advice which I took from Bill Stoves and keep them safe for later. Oh, and by the way, if you are a supporter of a club, take the programmes home. All the best!

Players in Football I Know

When, as a manager, you are offered to take over another club in a higher league, you must do your homework, before you make your decision, especially in non-League football. If you had to make your decision as a League manager, in a professional club, would you be concerned about the fact that the club who want you finished fourth bottom of their League and just survived relegation by a couple of points? How would your list of questions, when interviewed, pan out? Would it be the money in your bank over the nine or so months you work? Or would it be the money the club would give you to spend to bring in new players? Or if you were already happy with your staff at the club where you were working, would you want them with you, at this new club, possibly or definitely? How well do you know the players at this proposed club? Have you phoned friends to ask about the club you may join, especially if they have spent time at this club recently? If you have a family with children already in school and you are living in an area which means a move of over 100 miles for the family, you are moving away from friends and, sometimes, relations. You have to do your homework on the players you are going to manage. And when you make your decision, after you have been given 48 hours to do so, you agree to join the club, not having enough time to know what future lies ahead.

Your family has to be 100% behind you, even when they know their lives are going to change. New friends have to be made locally, in schools and for after-school enjoyment. The good thing is that your children's friends can bring their parents together with you and they become friends, after a while.

Yes, you are being paid well, but that allows your new club to take control of holidays, spare time and responsibility for your job, day and night. Someone I know in football took on the job offered and while he did a good job, the family he loved took a back seat, as far as being the most important people to him. That changed to the club being the most important people to him.

When you take in the important people in your life, in a manager's job at a professional club, that should always be your family, your job and the people you work with day to day. But how strong has your wife got to be, as she takes a back seat to your job? I wonder if your players could go through their short stay in football, as strong and loyal to you and your family, as your wife? If they did, you would not be fighting off relegation. You could be winning trophies.

Football the Game - What it Takes to Make the Grade

No doubt most footballers who play for their school team and play with their mates after school, then progress to play for a non-League club, dream of making the grade to play professionally. However, while enjoying playing, you all have a team you support, following them in the League and the FA cup and maybe, if your favourite players are chosen to play for their country, that gives you more belief that if you work hard, you could make it as your role-model has. Ambition has a big part to play in your progress, also ability and a certain amount of belief in yourself.

As for me, I felt at school that I wanted to be a footballer and progress to my district XI. I felt I was heading in the right direction. The fact that my dad was a coal miner, working six days a week and sometimes six nights, although days or nights, it was still pitch black when you worked 300 to 400 feet below the surface, meant he never got to see me play football until I was 24 years old. By then, I had joined the Army. Within a few months, I was chosen to play for the British Army XI, which to me, was an honour and progress, travelling to Europe to play in France, Belgium and Germany, at big grounds in front of big crowds and many others. However, there was a downside to this.

During my time playing for the Army XI, I was fortunate to arouse the interest of Swindon Town FC Manager, Don Rogers, Brighton FC Manager, Joe Wilson and Bristol City Manager, Alan Dicks. But to no avail, as the Army Sports Control Board would not allow me to be bought out by any of the clubs, yet no reason was given to me as to why I could not be bought out. Luck plays a big part in progress of any kind and my luck was not with me when I hoped it would be.

However, I did eventually make it as a professional, soon after I left the Army. While I was playing for Waterlooville under Jim Storrie, he was given the manager's job at St Johnstone and within a few months he asked Peter Faulkner, the Chairman at Waterlooville if he could take me to his new club on a long-term loan. Peter agreed and Ron Stanton, a director at Waterlooville, picked me up from Jubilee Road at 5 am on the Saturday morning, which was the starting date of the Scottish League, and flew up with me to Glasgow. We were picked up at the airport and the taxi drove us to the Argyle Hotel, where St Johnstone were staying before their start of the season against Glasgow Rangers, at the Ibrox stadium.

So don't ever give up on your dreams and ambitions to be a footballer at whatever level you achieve. Yes, I had a weird, yet wonderful day, to begin my professional career. On the Wednesday before my flight to Glasgow, Waterlooville played Salisbury FC at Jubilee Road and in front of 2,000 fans, we won 3-0. On Saturday, I was playing at Ibrox against Glasgow Rangers, in front of 50,000, starting in the number nine shirt. Even though we lost to Rangers, I loved every minute of that day, my professional career. So don't ever give up on those dreams and ambitions, because sport at any level, when taken seriously, is well worth the effort, and the pleasure is your reward, whether as an individual or as a team player and, as you know, due to the effort you put in when your mates are more interested in the girls, the girls become interested in you.

My Achievements in Football

When you, as a person, become proud of your achievements in life and humble within your character, you will be looked upon with respect by friends and relations, but more so by your opponents in your chosen sport. Football is a team game and when things are not going right for your team, it is easy to point the finger at those who have made mistakes during the 90 minutes. Managers who point the finger at players who may have contributed to a defeat can do it in many ways. Some will use expletives, shouting and pointing directly at the players involved, and some will explain it in football terms, without picking on one player. As a manager, you find that method will be more positive to help the team gain the three points. You can always put it right on the training ground.

I found that to be the correct way, not to blame one player, as long as you can highlight the mistake when coaching. When working as an assistant, who has been in both non-League and professional, you find various ways to make your point when explaining what you want, whether to an individual or the team. While working under Gerry Armstrong and Alan Mullery, I realised the right way. Both top internationals chose to talk to the individual, while walking out for the second half with the player on one arm and the team captain on the other, explaining what they wanted.

When I look back on my career in football, my achievements will not match the likes of Sir Stanley Matthews or Cristiano Ronaldo, but to me they are my achievements at my levels, as a player, a coach and manager, spanning 60 years in football.

If you look back at your achievements, or if you are still involved in the game, then to you, they are very important at any level. Your trophies will allow both family and friends to show how successful you have been. You will feel proud at the individual trophies and team trophies you have in your cabinet, for the game you loved and would have played come rain, snow and, dare I say, carrying a slight injury, which we should keep quiet about.

The game of football has the greatest following of any sport in the world, as a supporter, a player or a manager, and let's not forget the men behind the scenes, i.e. the chairmen, directors, groundsmen, trainers and physios, among whom today women play a big part in football at every level. The standard of women, at all levels, has progressed immensely, from non-League to professional and to international level. They should all be very proud of their achievements. Thank you football!

At school, I played up-front in the number nine shirt and represented the district at county level.

At the age of 16, I joined the Army Boys' Training Unit and moved to Troon in Scotland, where I was invited to train with the Scottish team at Largs on the west coast, prior to their game against Poland at Hampden Park ,and was invited to the game.

When I finished my army training, I was posted to Cyprus and joined 42 Squadron RCT. We won the League and Cup. After six months serving with the United Nations, I was transferred to Aldershot and soon afterwards I was drafted to Northern Ireland, where on our few days off, we organised a match, at which both Denis Viollet, Manager of Linfield FC, and Gibby McKenzie, Manager of Portadown FC, approached me and our CO to ask if they could sign me and buy me out of the army.

On my return from Northern Ireland, I was posted to Salisbury and was asked to travel to Aldershot to have a trial for the British Army XI. I was chosen to play up-front and that was the start of my many games for the army and the combined services.

It was during this period that Don Rogers, Manager of Swindon Town asked the Army if I could join Swindon Town and Joe Wilson at Brighton and Hove Albion, also asked if I could join them. Also, John Mortimer came up to Aldershot and told me that Portsmouth would like to sign me.

Now for those who don't know, the Army has a Sports Control Board who decide on anyone leaving the army before their service is completed, by a club buying that person out. Well, for some unknown reason, every club who approached the Sports Control Board to buy me from the Army was refused. On one occasion, I was playing for Winchester City at their old ground, Airlie Road, against Basingstoke. After the game I was called over by the Bristol City Manager, who was standing with our Manager, Jack Norris. His offer to Winchester was £10,000 for me to join him at Bristol. Jack Norris then explained that I was still in the Army and Alan Dicks, who was a perfect gentleman, said he would write to the army for permission to ask for me to sign, but the answer was no.

In the 1973 season, playing for the RCT Depot, we won the Army Cup at the Aldershot stadium, Queens Avenue, along with five other senior trophies. It was, without doubt, the most successful season to date for Depot. When I left the army in 1975, I joined Waterlooville, playing, and had a very successful season. After the season had ended, as I said earlier, Jim Storrie wanted me at his new club, St Johnstone in Scotland, for the start of the new season. A deal was agreed and I played in the opening game of the season against Rangers at Ibrox, after signing my first professional contract, while my wife and children were living in 51 Jubilee Road.

On my return to Waterlooville, after a very enjoyable time at St Johnstone, not only was I back with my family, but I felt a lot more comfortable, yet grateful to Jim McKinley, Jim Storrie and my team mates at Muirton Park. Also, Jim Peacock, our trainer and Scotland physio.

In the late 1980s and with a few more trophies, I received a letter from the Army, asking me to attend a presentation evening at the Officers' Mess in Aldershot. I read the invitation and returned the slip on the letter, saying I would attend the evening. Arriving at the Officers' Mess, I was met at the door by my Commanding Officer, Major Coan, showing me to my seat on the top table, with an empty chair either side of me. Within ten minutes, all of the chairs on the top table were full and I had Bobby Charlton, the footballer (now Sir Bobby) on my right and Henry Cooper, the British Heavyweight boxer on my left.

All tables were full and the Master of Ceremonies gave the regimental band the order to play. After some five minutes of music, the presentation was awarded to me. Now I need you all to know that Sir Bobby and Henry Cooper served in National Service for a maximum of two years, while I served almost nine years. The presentation was for the sportsman who had achieved the most in the Army, in the Royal Corps of Transport. To this day, this was my most honoured achievement and I couldn't apologise enough to Sir Bobby and Henry.

Coming to the later stages of my playing career, I was asked by both Portsmouth and Southampton to play in their ex-professionals team and travel to areas in and around Portsmouth and Hampshire to play in charity matches, which I really enjoyed, as I could take Ann to watch the games, mainly on a Sunday.

Then one day, my phone rang and it was Peter Osgood, asking me to play for the Southampton ex-professionals in a competition in France for over-38-year-old players. I said yes, after a chat with Peter and a chat with Ann. We were to meet on the Thursday, early evening and pick up the coach en-route. When I climbed into the coach at Waterlooville and was introduced to the players, I felt a bit awkward, as there were internationals and top players taking their seats: Jim Steel, Jimmy Case, Bill Beaney and Peter Osgood, to name but a few. When Peter introduced me, only Jimmy knew me. Jim Steel, who ran a pub, went into the services and bought large bottles of coke to mix with the vodka and gin which he had brought from the pub. So it was drinks all round, then we were on our way to the ferry at Dover.

We arrived in France and the hotel where we were staying had all the other teams' players and staff staying too. As soon as we had checked in and found our rooms, the only thing we all wanted was to fall onto our beds and have a couple of hours' sleep. However, one of the competition organisers reminded Peter that our first six-a-side game was a 2.30 pm kick-off and the tournament area was three miles from the hotel. We had to be there to check in at 2 pm. Peter, our manager, told us to be at the entrance to the hotel for 1.30 pm. After an hour's sleep, we assembled outside the hotel entrance and were on the bus and ready. The venue was very impressive, with marquees, stalls and two seven-a-side pitches looking very good. Peter checked us in and we went into the changing room to prepare. We were ready to walk over to the pitch, when the local band started to play the National Anthem, then the Belgium Anthem. On the pitch, we smiled and clapped the band off. The games were 20 minutes each half and we came off winning 3-1. I managed a couple of goals and on the way back to the dressing rooms, I was stopped by a reporter, asking me about the game and the team.

When I got back to the dressing room, my suit, shirt and shoes had gone. I came out, looking for someone to ask, but by then the lads had moved to the beer tent. Still in my Southampton strip and boots I found the tent, and saw the lads with their trousers, shirts and shoes on. I asked them where my gear was. A few lifted their shoulders, saying 'Search me', while Peter said 'Go to the lost clothes tent and ask there.' I went looking for the tent for some 20 minutes, but to no avail, so I walked back to where the boys were, asking if any of them had seen my clobber. Still a no was the answer, but a couple of the lads were being too quiet, allowing me to feel as if they knew. Not having any money I asked Peter for a drink, and he gave me enough to buy a coke. While walking back to where the boys were, I noticed a tramp wearing what looked like my suit, etc. I ran to him, telling him he was wearing my clothes. He shook his head, telling me in French, which I couldn't understand, that they were his, so I dragged him to the changing room, while passing the boys on the way, all laughing and applauding. I made him take my suit, shirt and shoes off and gave him my Southampton shirt, shorts and socks, and he was chuffed.

My clothes smelt a bit, to say the least, but I walked to the table where the lads were and they were hysterical, while Peter told me that they had written a sign saying 'for sale' in French, at five francs. This tramp came along and bought them, going to the changing room, then coming out with my clothes on. This was the kind of thing team mates got up to on football outings and yes, I saw the funny side of what the lads did. Brilliant!

There was talk in the press that Wembley stadium was going to have an update, both internally and externally, with the FA taking over the stadium from Brent Council at the time. Brent Council said they would have a final match for charity, prior to the handing-over. The game was to be between an Ireland XI, selected by Gerry Armstrong, and an England XI selected by Peter Osgood. Peter's side included Alan Ball, Alan Hudson, Jimmy Case in the middle of the park and me up top. So the pressure was on for me to get a result from the service I was going to get.

We went in at half-time 2-1 ahead and I managed to get a goal, but when we sat down, Peter did his manager's job, so that we knew what he wanted. He then said 'Does anyone want to add anything?' I put my hand up and Peter said 'Yes Robbo?' So I turned to Alan Ball and said 'Alan, knock the ball past their centre-backs, as I can beat them for pace.'

Well, Alan looked at me and said, 'I won the World Cup here, amongst other trophies, and you want me to knock the ball into space? I have never passed the ball into space, I pass it to feet and I find that an insult. Have you ever seen me play?' 'Well, yes,' I said and I knew I was out of order. 'Sorry for asking' 'I said. Alan looked at Peter and in his squeaky voice and with a smile said, 'I will let you off this time, but don't forget who you are playing with.'

Out we went, for the second half, and I managed to score a second goal from a pass from Alan. He turned away saying, 'Bloody amateurs!'

We came off, winning 4-2. After shaking the Irish players' hands, I went to apologise to Alan and a smile was all over his face. Before I could say sorry, he said 'What do you think and how do you feel after playing and scoring at Wembley?' 'Great' I said. 'Well, now you can say you played with Alan Ball, oh and by the way, I've played here over 20 times, for club and country', with the biggest grin on his face.

It left me realising the difference between Alan Ball and John Robson. Thanks, Alan, and thank you football for making my dreams of playing and scoring at Wembley come true. I just wish my dad had been alive and able to see me.

My CV

I acquired my FA Coaching badges while serving and playing for the British Army XI until 1974, when I had served my time of nine years.
1974-75 season I signed for Waterlooville Football Club.
1975-76 season I signed for St Johnstone in the Scottish Division 1.
1976-80 I came back to Waterlooville in the Southern League.
1980-81 season I signed for Farnborough Town FC in the Isthmian League.
1981-82 season I signed for Bognor Regis FC.
1983-84 season I was player-coach at Eastleigh FC.
1984-85 season I joined Fareham Town as a coach.
1986-88 I signed as Manager and player for Petersfield, winning promotion to the Vauxhall Opel League.
1988-89 season I joined Steyning FC in the Sussex Senior League and played in the Senior League Cup Final.
1990 joined Southwick FC as the Coach and assistant to Alan Mullery.
1991 I signed as assistant to Gerry Armstrong at Worthing Town FC, winning promotion in the first season as Division 2 winners.
1994 Gerry Armstrong left Worthing FC to take the Manager's job of the Northern National Side and I was asked to take over as Manager of Worthing Town FC.
1994 season we won promotion to the Isthmian Premier League and reached the first round proper of the FA Cup, playing Bournemouth away, losing 3-1 and finished the season winning the Sussex Floodlit Cup for a second time.

My Parents and Me

My Mam and Dad

Dad and me

My sister Rosalind and me at Blackpool

Me

Mam and Dad at Blackpool with me aged 7

My Family

Ann and me Wed in May 1969

My young family: me, Ann, Darren, Lisa and Scott

My family when they were a bit older: me, Ann, Darren, Lisa and Scott

The Army and Me

Winning the Cyprus Cup

Me in Cyprus in 1968

Our team in Cyprus in 1968

Trophies : King's Cup   Jubilee Cup   Army Cup and Replica   South East District Cup   Aldershot Senior League Shield

We won several Cups in the Army

Football and My Friends

Beau Reynolds,
Worthing Chairman

JOHN KILL
Centre back John is in his second spell at Jubilee Park, playing in the promotion team before moving on to broaden his experience with Southern League rivals, Bognor and Basingstoke. Twenty seven years old, he was capped at England Boys Clubs level, twice making appearances against Wales. John is a director with a building company and lives in Waterlooville.

John Kill who passed away after being hit in the chest by a football.

John ROBSON
Manager. A vastly experienced and well-respected Manager and Coach, whose past Clubs include Eastleigh, Bashley, Winchester City, and Worthing, among others. John has led his Suburban League side to become Champions of the Southern Division with six games in hand. At the time of writing, John's squad are unbeaten in the League, taking maximum points in all but one match. His fondest memories of his playing career include scoring twice in a

KIM MANNS
Kim has been at Waterlooville off and on for six years, since he was a 16 year old. Pompey took him on the staff when they re-started their youth policy and he was a professional there for six months, captaining the youth team. Poole Town was his next club but his stay was only short and he came home to Waterlooville. Kim is a striker, and at 22 is a burglar alarm engineer. He lives at Hambledon.

Kim Manns who we lost years ago through illness

Suburban League Challenge Cup Final
Salisbury vs Dunstable Town - April 2008

Football and My Friends

GOFF WHITE
Wholehearted Goff is a centre forward in the traditional mould — strong, aggressive and a man who never gives less than 100 per cent. Joined Ville three seasons ago, he has made several Southern League appearances and scored a memorable goal in the opening match against Guildford. Previously played for Ryde Sports after a spell on Pompey's books as an amateur.

Goff White lives in Basingstoke and is still my mate

Bobby Stokes and Janet on holiday in Spain with Ann, Scott and me

Worthing Football Club,
Me, Beau Reynolds with Morty Hollis, the Club President

Football and My Friends

Roy Beazley MBE

Albert McCann

Jeremy Stagg, The Best

Tony Cox

Football and My Friends

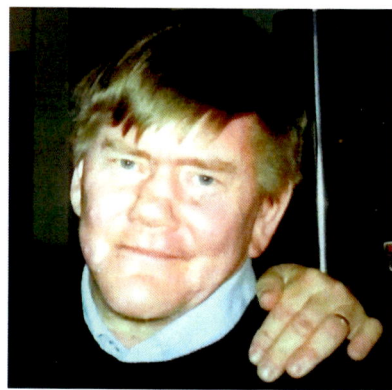

Roy Smith,
Blackfield and Langleys Supporter
RIP

Peter Osgood

Dave Leworthy at Spurs

Football and My Friends

Cliff Huxford, a true football friend
RIP

RICHARD DAMERELL

Richard has been at Waterlooville since the 1970-71
season, showing consistency
and occasionally brilliance
for both the first team and
reserves. Shares goalkeeping
duties now with Trevor
Gilbert who is the first to
acknowledge his friendship
and advice. Richard was with
Fareham United in the
Portsmouth League and had a
year with Hampshire League
Gosport. Twenty five year
old Richard is a gas technician
and lives at Bedhampton.

Richard Damerell, our goalkeeper at
Waterlooville

Jamie Bray with me as the Assistant Manager
at Andover Town

1996 I took over as Hampshire Senior Youth Team Coach, reaching the quarter-final of the county championship, losing to Worcester County.

1999 season I took the Manager's job at Alton Town FC, winning the Hampshire League and reaching a record number of points, but the club was refused promotion, due to the Bass Alton ground failing to reach safety standards.

I then left Alton to join Camberley Town FC for the 1999-2000 season, finishing in the top half of the League and reaching the Senior Cup Final at Aldershot's ground.

I returned to Alton Town after players, staff and supporters had all worked on the ground, making sure it was up to the standards required to win promotion for a second time. We finished the 2000-2001 season winning the League and gaining promotion to the Wessex Premier League and in the FA Cup, beating Sutton United away from home, some 60 places higher in the leagues.

In the season 2002-2003 I joined Winchester City FC, run by the Chairman, namely David Malone. Five months after putting a side together, in August, we were unbeaten in all competitions, playing 35 league and cup games, winning 34 and drawing one game. Yet on my way to take training one Tuesday evening, my phone rang and it was the Chairman, asking me to call in and see him. This I did and looking down on his paperwork, he mumbled the words, 'I am dismissing you, because you are not the right man for the job.'

Given our results and the games to come, I knew our players were loving every game, so I took training with Neil Hards, my assistant, and before they went for their showers, I got them all together with Neil to tell them I had been sacked. To a man, they all looked at me with dismay, then said I was joking. I said, 'Neil will be taking over.' When I had said it, Neil said, 'If he has sacked you, then he has sacked me.'

'No,' I said, 'just think of this squad we have here. Carry on and clean up, Neil. These players are special.' And with that, I told them to carry on together. This they did and were successful, winning the League, the Senior Cup and the FA Vase at the end of the season, at St Andrews in Birmingham. I still feel proud, no matter what.

I'm sorry to say that I went to Cliff Huxford's Celebration of Life on Wednesday 15th August, 2018 at Wessex Vale Crematorium, Southampton. Cliff was a very good friend and the first manager to phone me when I left the army. At that time, he was the Manager of Basingstoke Football Club and I signed to play for him.

Today showed how liked Cliff was, given the number of people present, family, friends and footballers. The Life of Cliff allowed everyone to know how special he was and that a big part of his life was taken up with football. Cliff played for Chelsea and Southampton, making some 360 appearances for both clubs, then went into management. You will be missed by all who knew you, Cliff, due to your honesty and experience in football and as a gentleman in your everyday life. Thank you for being a friend.

Nick Holmes, the manager, invited me to join Salisbury FC as a coach. I said I would, but if another job as manager called, then I would consider joining them. Nick agreed and after two months of working alongside Nick and Tommy Widdrington, both Newbury and Totton FC offered for me to take over as manager. I considered the travelling, and the players I knew at both clubs, and chose Totton. We finished third in the League and won the Wessex League Cup, beating Eastleigh in the final.

I left Totton, as Nick Holmes asked me to come back as coach, working with Simon Browne, running and managing a new team, which they had entered into the Suburban Football League. Simon and I had a choice of players from both our youth team and reserves. We formed the squad and finished the season, both winning the League with three games left and then beating Dunstable Town in the Cup Final at Imber Court, unbeaten in the League.

Our team was: James Bitter GK, Tom Clifton-Harris, Paddy Kinsella, Simon Browne, Joe Fisher, Chris Wheedon, Charlie Knight, Mikey Harris, Jamie Barron, Lewis Benson, Josh Rees-Long, Marco Tenten, Nick Watt, Danny Young, Jonathan Davies, Stuart Gates and Nathan Jones. I have said earlier, it's players who win you games. Managers play a part.

After really enjoying both periods working for Nick Holmes at Salisbury, I was offered a few jobs, one being at Laverstock and Ford. The Chairman asked me if I could work alongside their existing manager for a couple of months. Football had been good to me, so I agreed to help out, as they had just joined the Wiltshire League. As I said, I would do the job as assistant for two months, which I did.

Soon after, I did some scouting for Dave Diaper, who was Chairman of Sholing. While all this helping out was going on, I received a call from my friend Craig Davis, asking me to come to Fleet Town, where Craig was a player-manager. I went down to watch for a few games, then got involved on training evenings, giving my opinions on certain aspects of their game and how I felt they could do better. Craig gave me a free hand, so I could talk to his players and explain in training how to cut out some small mistakes. I enjoyed working alongside Craig and his staff and collectively we had made them a better side, both with and without the ball.

After my spell with Fleet Town and Craig, I went to Alton Town, my old club, trying to give them guidance in their new League. Many managers and coaches will disagree with me when I say that it is players who win games and yes, managers and coaches play their part in preparation. Also, referees and their assistants can lose you the points on a bad decision. But players, over the 90 plus minutes, play the biggest part in deciding the outcome. Is there a difference between non-League and League football? Yes, it is based on ability, attitude, fitness and the amount of money you earn. Contracts play a big part in League football, as players play various lengths of time at their chosen club. Outstanding players usually sign at top clubs for three or four years, depending on their agents, who in my opinion, can earn enough on the back of their player by 'upping the ante', as they say.

It has just come to light that all Premier League clubs can survive, even if they play in an empty stadium. This I cannot believe. The success of the sides and clubs, when it comes to playing football, relies on the supporters raising the players when things are not going too well, or controlling the side who is leading against their side, with their witty songs. If they could survive playing in empty stadiums, then allow supporters to attend free of charge!

Is it the money in football which needs addressing, or are there more things we need to look at? Some three years ago, I decided to travel around the non-League clubs to hold an open forum, asking clubs, including supporters, players, Chairmen and staff, to make our game a better spectacle. But it never got off the ground. This was my letter.

March 2015

Dear Clubs,
Can we, as chairmen, directors, officials, managers, players, both men and women, spectators and volunteers make the game we love a better spectacle for all?

My intention is to hold meetings at as many non-League clubs in Hampshire as possible, having an open forum, covering all aspects of our game, allowing opinions and ideas to be heard and discussed by everyone present, hoping we all can, in some way, help our games to be a better spectacle for all involved, from the chairmen to the spectators, without taking the help and commitment from us all. There will be no charge for the evening. All I ask is that, if you feel, as a club, this would help, then choose an evening to suit your club, from 7 pm start until 9 pm Mondays, Wednesdays or Fridays, inviting all participants involved with your club. I will reply to all clubs interested and hope to attend you all.
Yours in Football

John Robson

Meetings to commence from April, Monday 6th or Friday 10th and any Monday or Friday after these dates. You choose. Thank you.

John Robson
Please answer by letter. Thank you.

Making the Game more Honest and a Better Spectacle
I can never remember attending a training session at any level where the coach or the manager talked about diving in and around the opponent's 18-yard area, or defending a corner in our own 18-yard area, or where they said to the keeper and defenders, 'Go down if you feel an elbow or a push.' In training on set pieces against, you were told the opposite: win the ball, clear it and follow the ball out of the box. As a centre-forward I always came back as a defender, marking the opposition's centre-halves and ensuring he didn't score.

Having spoken to managers and coaches over the last five or so seasons regarding diving, or pulling someone by his shirt to stop him gaining the advantage, it's the players who decide what they do when losing the ball in their own half and that is where coaching comes into play. The player with the ball in your half and attacking your goal needs the nearest defender to the ball to close him down. If this doesn't happen, for whatever reason, then commit a foul outside your box, giving away a free kick, awarding yourself a yellow card from the referee, but allowing your team time to set up a wall and your keeper to make sure he is happy. Allow the player with the ball to get into your box, then tackling has to be perfect, no matter regarding the outcome, as the crowd will help the referee make his decision, along with his assistant.

We cannot please both sides in a football match; the decision given by the referee and his assistants has to be as honest and within the rules as possible, otherwise go to the screen, watch the action again and make the honest decision. It's right for the teams and the spectators, but most important, it is right for the game.

I realise that non-League does not have the cameras or screen available to help the referees make the right decisions. However, with technology and the speed it is progressing, I'm sure it won't be long before someone allows this type of assistant to help the referee with difficult decisions, while still having his assistant running the line for off-sides and throw-ins. They must stay, as they need the step-up to having the whistle and hopefully controlling the match themselves one day. Women assistants and referees play a big part in non-League football and some professional Leagues.

What, in my humble opinion, needs stamping out is the reaction when a player is tripped or fouled by the opposition and he decides to roll over six or seven times, e.g. Neymar. We all used to think this must be a bad one, on comes the physio, who has to give the impression he is repairing a broken leg, then helps the player off to the side-line; he then jogs on with the ref's permission, as if some miracle spray from the physio can fix every injury on earth, other than his honesty.

Let's take tackling to start. Has it progressed? Well, considering the pace of the game at all levels, the ability of defenders and midfield players when having to make a tackle has improved, but for those who, because of the lack of pace, find that pulling the opponent's shirt is the only way they can stop the player with the ball, can we stop this? In my opinion, if it happens more than once by the same player, he should be made to sit out of the game for a ten-minute period, the timing to be checked by the fourth official, and also shown a yellow card.

Tackling was an art which included timing, strength and awareness. We need these other methods of stopping a player with the ball removed from our game. Rugby has this punishment in its rules. Good rules, such as a goalkeeper having to clear a ball with his feet, as opposed to picking it up and killing the game for a short while, have proved to be a plus in keeping the game moving, while the new method of stopping the game when the referee needs to make a game-changing decision is something I find acceptable, as over a season a bad decision could mean a team relegated, due to a decision made without visual help.

I have often wondered if the referee and his assistant chat about decisions made during their game, which, when they watch the football programme on TV that evening, show the mistake which has allowed the teams to share the points, or when a team should have taken all three points. As Jimmy Greaves would have said, 'It's a funny old game!'

First of all, all supporters at professional level pay a lot of money to watch and follow teams all over, including the travelling expenses. No team has the right to win all three points, either at home or away. In all sport, when your team is home or away, whether it be rugby, hockey, basketball or football, in a team game, there are problems which happen during matches, like injuries to key players, players receiving cards in football and players in rugby serving time-out in the sin bin, which I would like to see in football; for a yellow card, say, ten minutes in the sin bin.

Bad decisions by the referee have more influence on the outcome of a game than the supporters in the ground. Yes, supporters can lift the atmosphere in a ground, which can lift players to perform, or their team to raise their performance. For me, most games will end favourably for teams who have suffered no injuries, or wrong decisions by referees, or better still, being the best team over the 90 plus minutes, but even teams who, on the day, play good, entertaining football and are worthy of winning a game, do not always go home with the points and praise for the way they played. Once again, as Greavesy said, 'It's a funny old game!'

How many games have you seen at grounds as a supporter, or on TV, or in highlights on Match of the Day and asked yourself, how did we lose that game?

Over the past four or five years, a manager has shown us a new winning way to win football matches and Leagues all around Europe. Is it because he buys the best players who can help towards winning games? Or is it the way he gets his team to perform? Or is it a method which he plays when his team has possession and also his organised defence, when his team don't have possession? How lucky are his Manchester City supporters, staff and players, while not forgetting they receive huge amounts of money, whether they win, lose or draw?

This led me to work out a mathematical cost regarding wages and supporters' outlay when following their team. Let us look at one of Manchester United's players. Given a crowd of 76,000, he could give each supporter a five-pound note towards their out-of-pocket expenses, both home and away. For me, it is in no way relative to the football an individual produces. What do you think?

Watching Football Today - Your Team

I agree, not everyone supporting teams is, or has been, a manager or coach with qualifications, having played at a high level. But supporters put their hands in their pockets week in and week out and sometimes take their sons and, on some occasions, their daughters, because they love their football and their club, whether they win or lose. What they deserve is effort and commitment from their team. To lose when your team gives total commitment can make losing easy to accept. Every supporter has the right to express his opinion verbally during the 90 plus minutes, given the cost week in and week out.

I should know this, as a follower of Sunderland Football Club.

I would not give my opinion regarding players or coaches and managers, as I rarely get to watch them these days, mostly due to the distance and also as I have been working in football for the best part of my life. I must say thank you to Sky Sport, BT Sport and Match of the Day. They keep me up to date, while I travel around watching non-League teams and doing the odd coaching and scouting job when asked, although I don't need to be working when visiting a game. Just to enjoy watching is enough, that is what football is about for spectators.

Making the Game a Better Spectacle

While writing, I have been giving the game I love a lot of thought, with regard to the money in the game, the massive financial earnings which players can get and the cost to supporters, who religiously follow their teams both home and away.

Well, if we go back a few months, I read in the sports columns of the bigger-selling newspapers that supporters make no difference regarding the financial upkeep of football clubs. That surprised me no end. Therefore, I sat and thought, first of all, if that is the case, let spectators in free. Then I thought the bigger clubs, which have grounds that hold more than 40,000 people, would suffer a large financial loss and that money would not help the non-League clubs looking for promotion.

As we all know, the better the season a team has, the more spectators start to fill the grounds, so how can we bring a team's followers in line with the game, knowing the gap between players who have contracts and get paid whether they play or not?

Regarding injuries, I'm not going to bring them into the financial outcome of missing games and still being paid, because some bad injuries can cost a player his livelihood. Just imagine, going into work on Monday and your boss saying to you, 'Sorry, but your standard of work has dropped, so we don't need you any more, I will be looking for a replacement.' Now, if you had an agreement and contract, you would receive the remainder of your contract as a lump sun, but it's not the same in all workplaces. Mind you, I am not a good example of someone who had quite a few contracts, but rarely read them before signing both the club's copy and mine.

Going back to making this wonderful game of football a better and cheaper game for spectators, as the clubs in the Premier League have stated they do not need the money supporters pay in order to fill the ground on match days. Well, let me tell you, you wealthy clubs, that if you played in empty grounds, our game of football would die a death within weeks. So, let me offer wealthy clubs, at all levels, an alternative to the millions of pounds your supporters, and the visitors' supporters, pay into your clubs over a season. Let us give something back to those genuine followers, who, week in and week out, pay to create the atmosphere which keeps this game alive, both home and away. Would my idea work, in professional clubs up and down our country? Here goes!

Making Our Game a Better and Less Expensive Game

To Premier League and Championship clubs, who reckon they can survive without spectators travelling and paying to fill their grounds, let us try this. At the turnstiles, there could be three alternative coloured tickets to choose from, costing five pounds each, but each supporter, whether home or away, only chooses one ticket on entry. Green is a home club win, yellow is an away team win, blue is a draw after 90 minutes, plus injury time. Winning tickets would have their five pounds returned at certain exits in the ground, if they wish. If not, then fine, but each club could have a registered charity to donate 50% of the money to. Most supporters would be getting a better deal, whichever club they support, if the ticket they asked for was not a winner, but the more relevant the charge for watching the teams playing, is pleasing to the pocket. It would allow friends who go with their mates, whether home or away, to have a small wager as to who would choose the winner on the day. I do feel that taking this option for supporters, both home or away, would see a rise in attendances at games.

I realise that some followers of their teams may find this a possibility to try, while others may scoff, but this could be a help to all spectators, but only to be used in League games, not Cup games or European games, obviously. We cannot bring into non-League games any ideas regarding the costs of travelling and watching teams, because they rely on their supporters and visiting supporters to help run the club. They only qualify for TV rights if they have a good run in the big trophies, like the FA Cup. Lincoln City proved that a couple of seasons ago, and well deserved it was.

Finance in professional clubs mainly comes from TV rights, or as is seen now, from foreign chairmen buying and investing in clubs and, I would say thank you for the money they invest in our top clubs, but the wages have to be brought to a sensible level, because it has become the main talking point amongst in our favourite sport.

If you ask your mates how much they earn over twelve months, £60,000 a year would be regarded as a fair amount, but the majority need to make sure they keep their job, no matter what. Now I would think that £60,000 would be around the average wage at the top flight of the Championship and Premier League, but remember, that is every week. Yes, they pay tax of around 40% on their income, but I am sure we wouldn't mind being taxed that amount on £60,000 a week, not forgetting advertising rights, etc. When you can't attend work as a professional, whether through injury or illness, your wages will still be paid into your bank. But don't forget you have a responsibility to each and every one who has given you the chance to work in front of both investors and those who pay to watch you for two games a week. That's three hours a week, with two 15-minute breaks, while your manager tells you you have collectively played well, or maybe not so well. Then it's back out for the second half of the game you love, knowing, win or lose, you have banked another taxable 60 grand in your account.

I have worked out that players in the Premier League whose transfer cost is a low 25 million are already millionaires before they even kick a ball for their new club, given their 10% of the fee. Yes, their agents will also demand a fee for negotiating their contract. Regarding the length of time you are to be a player for this new club, if we say that players have a career span of 15 years, then even playing in the Championship or Division One or Two, you will most certainly be comfortable about taking on a coaching or a manager's job, at professional level, or even dropping to the higher level of non-League football.

My Time at St Johnstone in Perth
Let me take you back to my spell in Scotland, in the 1976 season.

Once again, I did not read my contract when signing up for the club, with Jim Storrie, the Manager and Jim McKinley, the Chairman, present in the chairman's office at Muirton Park. I was only interested in maintaining a first team shirt, up front, for St Johnstone on a regular week in, week out, basis. Everything was going well, as I had played at Ibrox, before I had signed my contract, after arriving on that Saturday in August, for the start of the Scottish season. The first game for St Johnstone was away to Rangers. I started for St Johnstone, playing 85 minutes, then was replaced by Victor Robertson. We lost the game, but I really enjoyed it, after my slow start.

After I had been there for a month, I was asked to have a meeting with the Chairman in his office. The meeting was to ask me why I had not drawn any wages since I had signed. I explained that I had not needed to. He then explained that I was being paid weekly, including bonuses. When he told me the amount, I reminded myself that my dad was working six days a week as a coal miner, underground at the height of the seam, no more than 18 inches high and mostly on his back, with a light on his safety helmet. The wages he took home to my mam were £45 a week.

After my discussion with Jim McKinley, he advised me to send money home to those in my family who needed some extra money. With that, I agreed and we sent money to Ann and the children and my mam and dad. The Chairman did all of the necessary paperwork and I signed it and addressed it. I was at that time living in a private room in the centre of Perth, in the Salutation Hotel, all paid for by the club. That evening, I made phone calls to those who I had sent money to, leaving my wife until last, as I was phoning her almost every evening. I explained about the amount to my mam and dad and my mam was pleased. Just as I finished explaining, I told her how much I was earning per week and that my Chairman had sorted out all of the finance involved.

After a few months at the club Jim McKinley asked me if I would like to invite my wife up to Perth for a couple of days. Although I knew it would be great to see her, I didn't know why he had wanted Ann to come up. Ann's mam and dad had moved just around the corner from us and would look after the children for a couple of days. Ann sorted everything out down in Waterlooville, and within a couple of days she was with me in Perth. Jim McKinley picked us up and took us to a lovely area known as the North Inch, overlooking the sea and the Firth of Tay. He asked if we liked the area and the views. Our obvious answer was yes, as it was a lovely view. He then showed us a new four-bedroomed detached bungalow and said that if I would sign a new three-year contract, the bungalow would be my signing-on fee and would be ours to own. After looking at Ann, then the view again, I turned and asked my Chairman if we could discuss it between ourselves, when we got back to the hotel. Then I would give him my answer in the morning and say thank you for the offer. Ann also thanked Jim McKinley and Jim Storrie, who Ann knew from Waterlooville FC.

On our way to the hotel, Ann and I were quite quiet, apart from both of us agreeing that the bungalow and the views were exceptional, but we would need to bring the children and there was the fact that Alice and Jim, Ann's mam and dad, had moved from London to Cowplain to be near us and the children. I also discussed the move with some of my family in Durham and before Ann left to make the journey home to Hampshire, we agreed that the move wasn't for us. On Monday, when I got together with the two main people regarding St Johnstone Football Club, I explained my decision. They understood and thanked me for what I had done for the club. The following week, I flew home.

Football in 2018 at All Levels

Having been fortunate to be involved in football at all levels, i.e. playing at school football, youth level, county, non-League and professionally, with this experience, I feel I am allowed my opinion on this game, which is loved across most of the world by players, coaches, managers and, most of all, the spectators, who may also be involved in football at many levels. Now, opinions regarding football, at all levels, will vary from person to person, not forgetting that women are playing today at all levels and, hopefully, if they read this, are also allowed their opinion.

First of all, finance, i.e. my way of saying 'payment to players', yes, the earnings at all levels.

I think we would all agree that at Premier level, and those who are relegated, yet still have agreements in their contracts, are paid far too much money, considering their talent and hours given to the club over periods of two or three seasons, which will have bonus structures as extras for success during their time at the club. I do know that if a player and his team are relegated, then his contract will be reviewed accordingly, to suit the drop to a lower standard. Mind you, his income per week would surpass that of all supporters at the top levels, even after their tax deduction. While I realise these overpaid players at the top levels have accountants, and agents, they become millionaires after a couple of months at their clubs. The agents also claim their percentage, while negotiating the move for the player. I seem to remember the Manchester United midfield player, Juan Mata, attempted to raise money for charity by giving 1% of his wages each month to selected charities, which over a season would have raised thousands for numerous charities. However, as yet, I feel it did not get off the ground. I hope I am wrong when I say it, and I know that there are many of the top earners, both men and women, who do a lot for charities, but this was a no-brainer as they say.

Well, enough said regarding overpaid players and, while I know that you can't pay everyone the same wages in the top leagues of football, give a thought to the non-League managers, who prior to the season ahead are given a budget from their chairman and directors, which has to be managed across the squad. We are all aware that the forwards who are goal-scorers usually find they are the top earners, then it evens out as you drop back to the rest of the squad, with even less going to the guys who keep the bench warm.

Let's go back lots of years, when eleven starters in a team were usually set out as four at the back, four across the middle, of which the two wide players were on the wing and two up-front. Now it is classed as progress if your full-backs can both defend and be your wingers, while one of your centre-halves drops off as a sweeper, which may not last very long, due to allowing the opposition to push up and not be caught offside.

Today, managers and coaches select their players to cover areas when their team have not got the ball, but can ask questions of their opposition, when they have possession, meaning their fitness levels have to be close to 100% for the 90 plus minutes. When we only had one player on the bench, the game was much slower, whereas now, most problems are covered by the number of players available as substitutes, while only being able to use three changes to the starting eleven. Today, staff at most football levels have physios to cover injuries, and coaches on the bench in the technical area, so that the managers can run changes, before making those changes. Usually, spectators know much better and may be right at times.

It's never easy being the one person who has to have the answers to every problem that goes wrong during the 90 minutes, especially when you are playing in front of a full house, at any level, and everyone is expecting a positive result. But, I am afraid, it doesn't always happen the way you want and there are a few reasons why things are not going the way you expect them to, e.g. refereeing decisions, players looking a bit off their game in certain important positions, chances not presenting themselves in the attacking third; and the system you choose to play against the opposition, after having them watched, prior to them coming to you, maybe isn't working.

Those are just some of the problems that this wonderful game of ours is asking you, as a manager, and you don't have that much time to come up with the answers. Well, no-one told you this was easy! It's great when you are winning, but when you can't stop the slide, you take the problems to bed with you and everyone knows when you are struggling. When those around you try to help, that makes if more difficult. Go back to what got you to this point and work out what you have changed. Have you players who are not performing for you? It isn't an easy job, as a manager, but stick at it as best you can, if you are allowed, that is.

The Game in General

I do realise how fortunate I have been regarding football, yet not when I served in the Army. While serving in Aldershot some big clubs were offering to buy me out of the Army, none of the approaches came to fruition, although I did get to play at some big grounds in Europe, in front of big crowds, for the British Army XI. But I needed to test myself at a higher standard on a regular basis.

When I had left the army, the chance came along, while playing for Waterlooville, when I was asked to sign for St Johnstone, in the top division in Scottish football. Yes, it was a much better standard and I seemed to fit in quite well, but my family were hundreds of miles away, which meant not seeing my wife, Ann, and my young children growing up, on a daily basis. This was not easy for me, even though I was living the dream as they say. I do understand from my limited experience, that today in the Premier League when players are signed from European countries and sometimes further afield, that even with the money they earn and the apartments they live in, they must feel very much alone after a while. While I realise it is the top flight in football, when they are called back to play for their countries and are given time to meet up with their families, the next day they are back on the plane home, win, draw or lose, talking with team mates about the game, while part of their mind is thinking of their family and wondering when they will see them again. You have to be strong while at your new club and even stronger when on the phone, in your apartment, alone.

The job you have is the job you dreamt about as a boy growing up, but I do wonder if some of the negative thoughts in your head don't allow you to settle into your new way of life, which, consequently, affects your job when playing. Staying strong, both on and off the pitch, is a must, but it must affect your game at times. Fitness, at the highest level, has to be at the top of your list for both training and games and when working during both, you must sleep well in preparation for each session and game ahead.

Does the money you earn help to ease the problem of being alone in the evening? Don't forget, as a well-known and recognisable person, going out with your team mates for a drink, even if you only have one, soon gets back to your club and manager, then you are in the office the next morning, or worse, you are in the newspaper. These things are the burden that new players coming to a big club from abroad have to take into account when trying to perform at the top level.

Let's talk about the non-League game, which many of you reading about football are involved in. Yes, there is a difference between almost every aspect of the two standards. First of all, everything, well almost everything, is done for you as a professional and what you must do is to maintain the standard which made you a professional, both in fitness and ability. Also, your attitude at the club-level should improve, given the every-day training sessions, of which you are a part, not forgetting that it is a team game.

Now, what has been said should be almost the same at the national level of non-League football, where clubs don't have the following through the turnstiles at home games, and when the club travels to away games, it becomes an added income to players if they drive along with, maybe, two or three players. Whereas, when it comes to representing your club as a professional you may travel from your home to the club on a Friday, grab a seat with your team mates in your sumptuous coach, which will take you and some of your staff to the hotel you are staying in prior to your match the following day.

But whether you are a full-time professional, being looked after by your club, or a non-League semi-pro, picking up your expenses, plus a few pounds to go out with your mates or the girlfriend on a Saturday evening, never forget, you are being paid to play for 90 minutes, for the sport you love, so don't give anything less than 100%, because in non-League football, you get to know most of your supporters personally, after the game in the club bar, when you are in the supermarket shopping, when you are visiting a friend or relation in hospital, and when you are walking the dog. They will always say hello and sometimes chat about the game yesterday.

But one thing you must not forget, these friends pay to watch you and your team mates on a Tuesday night at home, then travel to wherever you are playing away on the Saturday, League or Cup games, which means you go out onto the pitch and, when the referee blows the whistle to start the game, your responsibility is to give your best to team mates, supporters and your staff, from your chairman, the manager, the coach and physio. But that should be easy, as you are playing the game you love, football. How lucky are you?

Now, let's talk about those who play a big part in the outcome of a game. No, not the players, the officials, four in number at football's professional games and three, when you come down the ladder to the non-League County League games. Just to let you all know, the officials for Premier and our Championship matches, are very well paid indeed, however, they do have to work hard to get to that level and are subject to panels behind the scenes, deciding on who, and why, they should move up their table, towards the big games, then hopefully, to referee FA Cup Finals and travel abroad to referee.

Respect is a word which not many supporters or players and their managers allow referees and their assistants, i.e. linesmen. The officials take the complaints from both managers and, sometimes, players; those on the pitch and those on the bench. I come back to the game of rugby. Have a sin bin, initial warning, then minutes and a second warning, red card and off. I have a good friend, Alan Robinson, who was good enough to referee at the very top level, i.e. FA Cup Finals and international matches. He was always fair whether talking about clubs, players or managers. Regarding spectators, whether home or away, you can never please all supporters, but as Alan always said, running the game to try and please supporters was not on the menu.

Be fair to both teams and referee to the rules, with the help of your linesmen, sorry, referee's assistants. Yes, I favour new technology coming into our games, especially regarding whether the whole of the ball crossed the line and also whether or not a penalty should be awarded. For those who think it takes a while for the referee to get to the screen, then watch the replay and give the correct decision, I will remind you that some players look as though they have been hit by a truck, rolling about until the physio gets to where the injured player is lying, gives him a rub, then lifts him to his feet. He jogs away, with the physio's assistance. Then on he comes to carry on with the game. I only hope that these kinds of cons don't creep into women's football. If you are injured, yes, but given the time it takes for the referee to make an honest decision, the screen is good and the decision is honest. Yes, I agree with the new technology.

Hoping to Make our Game a Better Spectacle
A few years ago, I was invited to a referees' and assistant referees' meeting (I still call them linesmen) at St Mary's Stadium in Southampton, as a speaker, to give my opinions about those who make the decisions during the 90 minutes and longer. The hall was full of existing referees and assistants and also, some 15 or so

young lads training to become referees. I talked first of all about players and supporters, who take great delight in abusing the men who cover almost every blade of grass, to ask them, does it affect your game? Or is it only when a player is cautioned and he finds he should let you know how he feels about the decision you have just made, in favour of the opposition, especially a free-kick around the 18-yard box or a penalty kick for the opposition?

What we need to know is, could we do the job? Are we fit and alert enough to get all decisions right? No. So now, at the top level, we incorporate cameras and decision-making referees, sitting in a studio, miles away from the game itself, giving their opinion on what and why the decision needs their opinion. Has this new method helped the game? Yes, for very important decisions, as the game is so quick today and we have many players/actors, who want the fouls and elbows, etc., who spoil the honesty of the game.

I met the Referees' Association Chairman who asked me to give my opinion on today's football and to answer questions from the hall. The main thing which impressed me was the young lads with their fathers, who wanted to be officials, after successfully passing the rules and the regulations required to qualify as an official.

After speaking about how I felt regarding football, and telling some stories, I gave the young lads a question regarding Alan Shearer who started as a young lad at Southampton FC. The prize was a 50p coin on which the offside rule was explained on the back. To my pleasure, they all had their hands up, ready to give me their answers. The young lad who gave me the correct answer received the coin. I said, 'Use the coin to determine who kicks off or picks an end.' It made my evening. Thank you for the evening, Mr Mike Riley. It was a real pleasure.

I have often wondered what makes a boy, or young man, want to be an official. Is it because, as a lad growing up, maybe he wasn't as good as his mates who he played with, or was it because his uncle or father were referees or assistants in the game? Whatever the reasons are, I am pleased they do want to hold that whistle, or raise that flag, because they are needed in most countries around the world. They certainly do need the help of the new technology, in order to cover those difficult decisions.

While we are on the subject of officials, as supporters of your team, swearing at the referee won't make him change his mind over a decision and, whether at home or away, he has the character and honesty to give the correct decision, no matter what you are calling him. Why don't you put yourselves in his position? He is on his own, in his stand-out strip. Take it from me, every decision he makes, even with the help of his assistants, will be wrong to a percentage of the crowd. Just imagine going home after 90 minutes and realising every time you blew your whistle, someone watching did not agree with what you had given. Never mind the decision, just show respect for the man in charge.

The Price You Pay for the Game You Love

Football you love as a player has only one big setback, injuries. We can all put up with the odd knock during a game, but the bad injuries, when you are helped off by your physio, or worse, you are stretchered off: only you know the pain.

I really take my hat off to the FA when head injuries have to be checked as soon as they happen. I remember the Tottenham player, Fabrice Muamba, who stopped breathing on the pitch. A doctor who was watching the game came running onto the pitch and resuscitated the player. How lucky was that! Yes, we have all seen bad tackles, which can end up with the player who receives the tackle coming off worse and having to receive treatment for weeks. Then the manager, suffering the loss of who may well be a key player, has to find a replacement.

From professional to non-League, injuries do sometimes end players' careers. With non-League players it can also affect their jobs away from football. So, when signing for a club, if you have a contract, make sure you cover your injury, when your work is manual labour, or even take out insurance, paying it from the wages you earn playing football at non-League level.

The reason I advise this stems from the length of time you spend as a player, at which any game may end up being your last, whatever level you play. If you are a professional, then you should be covered at all times by your club contract, provided your agent makes sure that, for the length of your contract, any injury which does not allow you to carry on as a player covers your personal loss. If the same injury occurs during your playing days at non-League level, you may find your club will hold a testimonial game for you, inviting some well-known professionals to play, who may come on for 45 minutes or so. If this is publicised prior to the date of the game, that could be an honest way of helping out players whose games from then on can only be watched from the stand.

Speaking of your time as a player, I can only refer to the great Sir Stanley Matthews, who in his days as a right-winger found his opponents to be twice his size and weight. The only way they could stop him going past them was to get stuck into him, hoping to give away either a throw-in or a corner when they felt they had done their job. Yet Sir Stanley played on into his fifties for his clubs, both Stoke City and Blackpool FC. Was it because of his fitness or good luck? You tell me!

I was very fortunate during my playing days in not picking up any threatening injuries, although while in the Army and some weeks during the season, I was playing three games a week for my regiment, my corps side and the Army XI. After a while, I began to feel the stress on my calves and ankles. However, the Army side gave me an open invitation to attend the Military Hospital a day before big games, to receive two cortisone injections, one in each ankle, near my achilles tendon. At the time it seemed they worked, so I just accepted it as a bonus. Later, when I finished playing, I found that it had cost me dearly, health-wise, even when walking. Eventually, I knew this was the price I had to pay for the game I loved. I took good advice from Don Taylor, a very experienced physio, who served the first team at Southampton for many seasons. He explained about the injections I had received. Although they killed the pain I felt while playing, they would have an adverse effect as I got older.

The thing was, I could never blame football, as I wasn't forced into it, yet it allowed me to play in many countries in Europe, work in the USA coaching and play at Wembley, which was more than my dreams as a boy. Would I have made as many friends, some of whom were top-flight internationals, yet down to earth and humble? Some, I am sorry to say, are no longer with us, but are still remembered by me and I am sure they come to mind in the big games, when supporters say to one another, 'I bet so and so would have scored that chance'. Or 'I bet our old centre-half would have cleared the ball.' Or 'Our old keeper wouldn't have let that in!'

Yes, the supporters who have seen their club through the years will always mention their players from the past, while not realising just how much the game has changed over the years: the footballs, the boots, the fitness of today's players making the movement quicker. Mind you, many of the players who supporters talk about during a game from the past would still stand out today, as the real top class would adapt to what was asked of them.

To finish off this section, when you are young, the injuries you sustain while playing, because you receive good treatment, you tend to shake off and tell your physio and your team manager that you are OK to play, and if your manager feels you are needed in the starting eleven, then yes, you start. However the game pans out, you complete the 90 minutes, whether you win, lose or draw. You feel OK, you shower and join your team mates for a tea or soft drink and sandwich. Then, when you are travelling home, you feel the odd pain from the injury you have been receiving treatment for, the one where you told your manager you were fit to play, because you felt no pain, and here you are still feeling twinges of pain.

Take it from me, you do not keep playing with an injury that gives you pain and prevents you from playing and especially when you are having injections of cortisone the day before your game. I'm glad to say that this kind of treatment is not popular these days, because of the long-term problems as you age. In 2013 I was taken into the Queen Alexandra Hospital for a major operation on my ankles, when I was given numerous bone grafts to help me walk without pain. I spent five days on a ward, then came home and was bed-bound for eight weeks, using a wheelchair when I wanted to get some fresh air.

During my recovery period, one of the internal screws used to keep the grafts in place came free and protruded through the skin in my left ankle. That day I was back in the Queen Alexandra Hospital for another operation. The surgeon, Dr Billy Jowett, who had performed privately on some well-known footballers, carried out the necessary operation and afterwards showed me an X-ray he had taken.

His first words as I came around were, 'No more football for you John Robson! You need to take up a manager's job and sign on a coach to carry out the necessary training.'

So, I say this to players, 'Do not come back to playing until qualified club physios give you the go ahead to start light training.'
But only you know whether you are fit enough to start even light training. If you feel any pain, either during or after your light training session, stop and explain to your physio and, if need be, tell your manager how you are feeling, so he can authorise rest and more treatment, until you know that you are ready for selection. Don't pretend to yourself that it should be OK. It won't be, unless you can do the warm-up before the game and feel no pain after the game. Oh and by the way, yes, it was the cortisone injections that did the damage.

When You Come to the End of Your Playing Days
I was fortunate, while serving in the Army, to be playing for the them when stationed in England, although when I was serving in Germany, Cyprus and Scotland, football soon allowed me to miss the odd duty. While serving in Aldershot, I was offered the opportunity to take the FA Coaching courses. Knowing it would be a positive when I left the Army, my answer was yes and thank you to my Commanding Officer, Major Coan. When chatting about my offer, he told me that when he was a young lad, he was on Chelsea's books, but was released by the club, as his father made him join the Army, hopefully to progress to become a Second Lieutenant and work his way up the ladder to become a Major. He was an excellent CO by the way.

I did take my coaching badge and qualified through the FA, which I was to realise was a massive plus for later, when I was too slow to play the game any longer. I was very lucky to play when I left the Army and made the professional level in Scotland with St Johnstone, then came back to Waterlooville to the delight of Peter Faulkner, the Chairman and David Munks, our manager. He had been an England Youth Team Captain, then made his first division debut for Sheffield United at his club's ground, Bramhall Lane, against Aston Villa. Now, we don't all get to the dizzy heights that David Munks did. As manager at Waterlooville, he made us players realise what experience he brought to the club. He had obviously passed his coaching badges, yet was a good manager and a good guy, to boot. We only see each other at funerals these days, so don't get much time to chat, but think about what you want, when you are honest with yourselves, and know you can't continue to play at the standard you achieved. Yes, you can play Sunday League, but that invites injuries; injuries which may affect your work. Like myself, you may have a son or daughter, whose love for football and ability has allowed them to play for teams who may play on Saturdays or Sunday mornings, or both. Follow their progress and offer any help to their manager that he may need. It's a start.

I realise we all have different responsibilities in life, regarding the number of children we have, the jobs we do, etc. But when you are bringing up your children, allow them to choose what they want to do, after showing them the various sports, pastimes, hobbies, swimming or cycling, and whatever they choose, give them encouragement as a father. Yes, we would all love them to take up football, but with your experience, you can guide them in the right direction, while not pushing them, but allowing them to enjoy what they have chosen.

My Perfect Squad of 16
I have picked here players from the teams I have coached, managed, and played in:

Goalkeeper:	Dean Beale. *Mr Reliable.*
No 2 Right-back:	Kevin Brewster. *The best dead ball, free-kick taker, corners and penalties, while still being an excellent defender.*
No 3 Left-back:	Spencer Mintram, Worthing FC. *Strength, pace and, in one season, came up with twelve goals from left-back. Worthing FC had numerous clubs asking for trials for Spencer, but his only problem was ambition, or lack of it.*
No 4 Centre-half:	Joey Byrne, Blackfield and Langley Centre-half. *Never tried to show off, just went out and*

did his job. As we say in football, a 7 every game and lots of 'Man of the Match' awards.

No 5 Centre-half: Luke Dempsey, Andover FC. *Mr Reliable. Luke covered his team mates and goalkeeper without a word from the bench, other than a 'Well done, Luke!' Rarely misses a game and, like Joey Byrne, a 7 every game.*

No 6 Midfield: Liam Greene, Winchester City FC. *Left side of midfield, either centre in a three. More of a creator than a sprinter. A player you would want to take penalties and free kicks from anywhere in the last third. Not so good in the air, but with the ball at his feet, he saw everything and delivered.*

No 7 Centre-half: Ian Humble. Centre-half or holding midfield player. *Ian didn't need telling, his love for the game showed every time he played.*

No 8 Gary Green. *Gary had it all. Played the holding role, if you lost possession, but when you had the ball, he could assess if he could be involved in the attack. A big, fit player, reliable, who nobody bullied. An all-round athlete and intelligent footballer. In my front three, in a 4-3-3 system, I would need players who could stretch the defenders, take them on with the ball, commit defenders and see a goalscoring chance, or a team mate in a good area.*

No 9 Centre-forward: Andy Forbes. *Has to be able to score goals and demand both centre-halves mark and cover his marker. As a No 9, you play most of your game with your back to the target, therefore your movement has to be good, sometimes for yourself and, at other times, for your team mates, but should be geared to finishing chances, whether it be from*

	mistakes by the opposition or supplies from team mates. Andy Forbes is your man!
No 10	Darren Robson. *At No 10, just behind the front three, creating chances for your attacking players and taking free kicks, in and around the box.*

Then, on my left, in No 11 shirt, would be Davy Blanch (Army player). On my right-hand side would be Jeremy Stagg, No 7, the best non-League player I worked with. Every game he would be involved in our win or draw, but was not a player who you would criticise for any chances created by both Jeremy and Blanchy. They delivered every game.

Squad Subs:

Goalkeeper	Eddie Green, British Army XI
Centre-forward:	Steve Poulten, Alton Town
Defenders:	Sandy Brown, British Army XI
	John Armon, Basingstoke full-back
	Lewis Benson, Andover Town, Salisbury Youth Team and Salisbury FC
Left-back	Joe Wright, Andover

My bench players were all good enough to start, if an injury occurred prior to the kick-off, but the motivation, desire and ability was already there, in every player picked. If asked why I've not picked this one or that one, I've had a long time to think and prepare this squad. My squad.

I thought about memories and achievements, games that stand out, along with the players who the opposition would realise had all of my confidence to go out on to a pitch and deliver, no excuses. The result was the most important thing, at the end of the game. I hope you all understand, every one of you who played for me and the clubs I managed, was respected by me and the staff I worked with.

Thank you isn't enough to you players who were on the subs bench, since I knew if I had to change anything during a game, the players I brought on were going to give the team 100%. Thanks again, guys. As it is players who win games, all that managers and coaches do is to prepare the players for the next game. I had good staff and chairmen and directors, who carried out the running of the club superbly. I feel I was very fortunate, given the players and staff I worked with throughout my footballing life, apart from my last club which I will write about later in the book.

Eastleigh FC - Visit up North
I was Eastleigh FC Coach to Don Gowans at the end of the season when I arranged to take our players to the North East to play some friendlies and visit West Auckland FC, to see the World Cup, which they won in the early century. Two old boys told us the story.

My sister sorted out a hotel for us. Then, on the way back, after being invited to the end-of-season presentation, we found that the old trophy had been stolen. Obviously we became part of the investigation. To this day, I'm not sure if it has been found. However, we were cleared of any involvement and, to date, when I bump into some of the original players, we spend time talking about the eventful, yet excellent, weekend, up in Durham.

Spennymore also invited my close family to the end-of-season presentation after we played them in a friendly on our visit to Durham.

When we arrived, there were two tables laid out for the players and a table laid out for my close family. On both tables were large bottles of whisky and bottles of wine. The evening was excellent and we, the players, that is, all came back to the hotel chatting about the hospitality shown on our visit to the North East.

We left to come home on the Sunday morning after breakfast, because of work commitments on Monday, and we found the hotel had made up some sandwiches for the journey. As the lads had sobered up from the evening before, thank yous were given to everyone concerned for our stay up in the North East and my thank you to football.

Jamie Bray and Bayber - Final Pages
It would be wrong of me not to include the guys who work for Jamie, in his recruitment company. I drop in now and then to say hello and

catch up on football and they also do events, mainly charity, which are always organised so well, for all concerned, raising much needed finance.

While I was writing this, Jamie was on his honeymoon with Jess. Knowing him, wherever they went, he will be making new friends; Jamie is like that, given his sense of humour. Back to his boys, I'm sure they are keeping the company running smoothly.

The Final Whistle with No Extra Time

First of all, thank you for buying my book and, if you enjoy it and maybe find your name mentioned on a page, then give yourself a pat on the back. Thank you for all of your calls, telling me to write this life of mine, and chats when we have met or worked together or you have played for the same club, and to those footballers who have become managers, then asked me to join them as coach to the players they have: it has been my pleasure.

Also, can I thank the supporters throughout the footballing world and especially the supporters in England, where this wonderful game started, all those years ago. Think about it, we have all been players, we have all been supporters, we have all had our highs and lows and sometimes have been asked, 'Could you run the line for us, as the referee has not been able to get to the game?' So one of the linesmen takes the whistle; 'Could you take a flag please?' And you did and when you got home, you told mam and dad, or the wife, or maybe your mates, 'I ran the line today, at my boys' match.' But what you did was much more important than that. You actually helped a match take place. Why? Because of football.

Let's start with Sunday football. All over our country, weather permitting, there will be lads and men, and sometimes officials, all getting together for their Sunday League games, plus supporters, mates, sons and daughters. Yes, let's not forget the ladies, both young and not so young. Personally, I have attended women's games and also watched the higher level, playing for the well-known clubs in England and then going on to be internationals. The standard is excellent and, I am pleased to add, we don't see too much diving and pulling players' shirts, etc.

The next step in football is non-League level, from county to the National League. County Leagues possess some very good players, who can rise to the national League. Clubs in these levels get very good support, even away from home. Yes, as you rise through the leagues as an individual, you realise as a player, that the game, becomes much more professional at the top level of non-League football. Nevertheless I say that you, as a player, should always approach any and every game to give your best for the team, at every level, not forgetting the supporters who pay to watch, both home and away. If you cannot give your all to the game, either because of injury or illness, then you should not play. There are players in your squad who may not be as good as you, in terms of ability, but they will give more to your team on the day in terms of their attitude.

I do hope you have realised that in this section, I have not mentioned money. I mean the amount agreed to pay players to serve their club. Yes, the players pay tax and pay their agents, but to pay Premier League and some Championship players the money which will make them millionaires after serving three and four months at their club is, I believe, obscene.

No wonder, once the side has been chosen by the manager, those starting the game are fine and, given their wage structure, those on the bench are still going to be paid, whether they play or not and that will include their win bonus. No wonder our Premier League has more footballers and managers from abroad. Is it to be part of the so-called top league in world football, I wonder? How often do we win the Champions' League these days? Do the scouts from the Premier, Championship and Division One and Two, just jump onto an aeroplane to look at a goalkeeper, defenders, midfield players and strikers? Save the plane fares, just fill their cars with petrol or diesel and send them around England, Scotland, Wales and Ireland. It's cheaper and doesn't any club, manager or scout get it right most of the time?

Sir Alex Ferguson set the standard, by bringing Cristiano Ronaldo to Old Trafford as a young man, and Barcelona brought Messi over from Argentina as a boy. Don't wait until they are established as world-class players, bring them to your club, then coach them to become a quality player. Can you all remember a player called George Best? He came to Old Trafford at 15 years old, then went back home as he was homesick for Belfast. Sir Alex brought him back and the rest is history. Why have we only won the World Cup once? Come on you Premier clubs, they are out there, go and get them! You have almost four years to coach and allow their flair to come into their ability. Field a good England team, with some of the players who were very good for us in Russia, and new English youngsters, who by then will give us a chance to bring the trophy home, where it belongs. Our youngsters, under-17s and under-20s, have proved that, at world level, we are good enough. With Gareth Southgate in charge, I feel they will be given a chance.

When I look back on my life at 71 years of age, I realise just how fortunate I have been. My parents made sure I knew right from wrong and respected those we saw who were not as fortunate as myself and my two sisters, Rosalind and Anne. My dad, John, was a coal miner, underground, digging for the black stuff, which, at that time, was wanted all over the country for various industrial and domestic needs. My mam, Bessie, was a housewife, as most women were in those days, until the coal mines in the North East closed down, meaning that my mam had to find a job. She managed to get a job at Tricity in Spennymoor and my dad joined Black and Decker, an American company, also in Spennymoor, operating a machine.

Football didn't play a big part in my dad's life, especially when my mam had a stroke, which left her confined to a wheelchair before she was 50. My wife, Ann, and I had set up home in Cowplain in Hampshire, with our three children, when I received a call from my dad to say my mam had died, at the age of 50. The following day, I drove to my dad's in Willington, County Durham, to see my mam in her coffin, looking as though she was sleeping. It was then that my dad turned to me and said, 'She gave up on life son, as she felt she was a burden to us all.' Then we both gave her a kiss and said goodbye. My sisters and the families and friends were there at the funeral, to say their goodbyes to a wonderful lady, who always put her family and friends first. Thank you, mam, for everything you did for my dad, my sisters and me. You were so special!

When I was in the Army and my friends and I had a few days' leave, I would take four or five of us to Willington, to number 25 Canterbury Crescent, to stay over. My mam and dad never turned us away.

My mates loved it and respected my parents for their hospitality. That was my mam and dad, and my two sisters are the same, with our John, Rosalind's husband and our Anne's husband Geoff. How lucky are Ann and I? We keep in touch with our family on a regular basis, even though they are 350 miles up north from Hampshire. No problem, they are only six inches away on my road atlas!

Ann, my wife, was an only child, who sometimes reminds me how lucky I am to have sisters to visit and keep in touch with, something she hasn't got. Her parents Alice and Earnest, or Jim, to those who knew him, are no longer with us, but Ann and I have our two sons, Darren and Scott and our daughter, Lisa, who between them have given us seven lovely grand-children. They are very close to us as a family and in fact they live in Hampshire, so very near for visits.

As for friends, we are fortunate to have many, who have been close to us when times were difficult and also in the happy times.

Football has played a very important part in our lives, for which I am very grateful. Like many team sports, it allows you to realise that within a team, you look out to help each other and the same is to be said within your family. You are a team, so you look out for each other, no matter where you are in this world. Nothing will change regarding football, yet things change regarding your family and friends and have, in the past, for me. Spare a thought for the difference: with football, you have your substitutes, so make the change. However, in life, with family, you can't just make a change, but you will find your friends will be there to help you through. Thank you family, football and friends.

As I said my parents made sure I was brought up to respect those who weren't as lucky as myself and my two sisters. Respect has become a word in my thoughts, no matter who I meet, who I've played with, or against, in my life, in football or in life in general. None of us should accept that we are supreme as a person, because none of us is and you will not gain respect if you feel, and act, that way. Whereas, if you are honest and hold respect, you will allow those who meet you to speak highly of you when they are in conversation about you, to someone else. Also, those who haven't met you, when they meet someone who has, should get a good opinion of you.

Honesty and respect for those you don't know will make our world a much better place and an easier life for yourself. Whether you are a boy or a girl, a man or a woman, a coal miner, a joiner, a plumber, a secretary, or teacher, it is a lot easier to show respect and honesty to people, even if they don't return the compliment.

The Final Whistle with Two Minutes Extra Time

I could not miss telling you all about this! Where we lived, on our new estate in Willington, we had good friends and neighbours, but we also had the police around every day, checking the workers' sheds and tipper trucks, in case they had break-ins or vehicles stolen. At this time, my dad wanted to learn to drive the car he had purchased second-hand. After spending all he had on the old car, he found he could not afford the lessons to pass his test.

I was in Hampshire, with Ann and our children, when our phone rang. It was my older sister, telling me my dad was having driving lessons. 'Fine,' I replied, 'How is he doing?' 'Fine,' she replied. 'Who is his instructor?' I asked. 'Well, he has passed me a few times in the main street, but I don't wave,' she said, 'In case he loses concentration.'

This went on for about a month and my dad had been seen driving all over the county with his instructor, until one day, he was stuck in a traffic jam. The police were doing vehicle checks. They saw my dad's L plates and walked around to the passenger side and asked my dad's instructor about three times to open the window. Then the PC opened the door to find a dummy in the seat, which my dad had made as his instructor! Needless to say, my dad was fined £100 and not allowed to drive again until he was registered with a learner-driver company through the police. However, in court, the judge complimented my dad on the life-like dummy, prior to fining him and banning him from driving. My dad now sits in heaven, but he is still banned from driving!

Playing and Managerial Experience
1972   Qualified as a Full Badge FA Coach

1972	Basingstoke, Army & Combined Services	
1974-75	Player, Waterlooville FC	Southern League
1975-76	Player, St Johnstone FC	Scottish Div^n 1
1976-80	Player, Waterlooville FC	Southern League
1980-81	Player, Farnborough Town	Isthmian League
1981-82	Player, Bognor FC	Southern League
1983-84	Player/Coach, Eastleigh FC	Hampshire League
1984-85	Coach, Fareham Town FC	Southern League
1986-88	Player/Manager, Petersfield FC	
		Hampshire League

Promoted to Vauxhall Opel League

| 1988-89 | Player/Coach, Steyning FC | Sussex Snr League |

Sussex Senior Cup Finalists

| 1990 | Coach, Southwick FC | Isthmian League |

Assistant Manager to Alan Mullery of Spurs and England

| 1990-96 | Coach, Worthing Town FC | Diadora League |

Assistant Manager to Gerry Armstrong – Spurs, Watford and N Ireland

1993	Promoted to Manager
	Division 2 Champions 92-93
	Promoted to the Premier 94-95
	First Round FA Cup on two occasions
	Twice winners of the Sussex Floodlit Cup.
1996-1997	Hampshire Senior Youth Coach
1998-1999	Manager of Alton Town, Hampshire League Champions with record points. (Alton were refused promotion on the grounds of its facilities not being up to standard.)
1999-2000	Managed Camberley Town, finishing 10th in the Ryman League and reaching the Aldershot Senior Cup final, losing to Fleet Town.
2001-2002	Returned to Alton Town and won the League again, and were promoted to the Wessex League after working on the ground facilities.

2003-2004	Asked to manage Winchester City. I took the job and put a side together which went 35 games unbeaten in all competitions. However, the Chairman decided I was not the right man for the job, and asked me to leave the club. Subsequently the team went on to win the League, the League Cup and the FA Vase at Birmingham's ground, St Andrews, under the management of my number 2, Neil Hards.

Nick Holmes, the Salisbury Manager, asked me to coach the forwards, until another job came along, and after about three months I was asked to take over at AFC Totton. I took the job and we finished third in the League, and won the Wessex Cup.

In the September 2003-2005 season, I was asked to take over the manager's job at Bashley FC. I managed them for a season, and at the end of the season, Nick Holmes asked me to return to Salisbury, which I did, I took the Youth Academy for the first season. The following season I took the reserves in the Suburban League, which we won, winning 34 games and drawing one game in an unbeaten run. Also won the Suburban Cup beating Dunstable Town at Imber Court in the Final. In 2008 most of the staff, including Barry Blankley, Ian Harris and me, were told we would have to leave at the end of the season due to financial difficulties.

2009-2010	Scouted for Sholing FC in their new league, under the request of Dave Dieper the Manager, watching the opponents they were due to play, and players they were interested in.
2010-2012	I was asked to return to Alton Town as Manager. I took the job in January 2010 and made the decision to resign for personal reasons. Craig Davis, Fleet Manager asked me to help out for a few weeks as they were bottom of their league. I helped out for a month, and then travelled watching games in all non-League venues.

FRIENDS

I have been very fortunate in my footballing career, meeting lots of very good people, including players, coaches and managers, while not forgetting the chairman of the clubs I have managed. Is it football that brings these people into our lives? I think it is. My reasons are that you make friends in football; you don't see them for months, or even years at a time, then you come across them, and within minutes you are asking each other, 'Where are you now?' 'Which club are you with?' 'We should get together for a round of golf, or even a wedding.'

Ian Humble, Alton Town

When, as a manager, you take over a club, you get a chance to look at your squad on training nights. Prior to listing your players for Saturday's game, you chat with your assistant and get to know his feelings about the system you intend to play, whether home or away. After selecting your starting eleven for the game, you are then looking for a leader who is quality, given the league you are playing in, and also is respected within the club as a very good footballer.

I did have two players in mind, and I asked the staff what their opinion was, given that one of the players travelled a round trip for both training and home matches of 80 miles, while the other player walked to Alton's ground in approximately 20 minutes. I knew that whoever I chose, the staff would give their opinions on both players, who ticked all the boxes. I then asked the staff to go home after training, and said that I would ring them on Friday evening and ask again who should be Captain.

Before I called the staff on Friday evening, I had pencilled in my choice, wondering if they agreed. I made the calls. Half an hour later we had agreed to differ for lots of reasons, and I phoned both players to let them know my choice. Yes, I wanted a captain who didn't go around shouting orders at his players, who knew how to address referees during the game, and who knew the game tactically. Ian Humble was the choice.

A quiet lad generally, a good footballer with or without the ball, pulling his players about when we didn't have the ball; forming a good shape defensively, and leading by example, as they say, in today's football: A seven out of ten every game. Actually, I would rate Ian higher, given his responsibility for 90 plus minutes.

When I left Alton and decided to ease down for a short while, I found that Ian had moved to Horndean FC, and I decided to go and watch their home games, finding Ian in the team's defence, leading by example, as he knows no other way. In one game Ian took a bad knock in a tackle and was out for quite a while. I carried on watching Horndean under the leadership of Michael Birmingham, another good friend of mine, and a very good manager, asking him about Ian.

'He took a bad knock, Robbo, so I had to bring in someone at the back.' Within a couple of months I received a call from Ian explaining why he had decided to pack in his football, given that his work had stepped up a couple of notches in terms of his responsibility and even better was the news that Mrs Humble had given birth to a baby girl, Lois, which was great news. Work now became very important to Ian and his family.

Ian, to me, was a perfect human being and a gentleman, and to be born a 'Humble' for Ian was the perfect surname.

Thank you for being a friend, Ian.

Paul Whitaker (Army)

On 18th September 2018 as I sat down to write some more pages for my book, the time was 10 am and my mobile phone rang. I answered it straight away.

'Good morning, John, it's Paul ... .' I did not catch his surname, and before I could stop him, he carried on telling me about when we played football together in our Army days. It wasn't until we told stories, back and forth, about our times together, that Paul said, 'By the way, I am phoning you from Australia, John.'

Well, that made things worse. Now I'm trying to remember a Paul who is living thousands of miles away in Australia, who while I am listening to our times together almost 50 years ago, I am desperately trying to put a surname to. He was obviously a very good friend and a very good footballer when we were together in Aldershot all that time ago. Then, after what seemed a lifetime on the phone, I said,

'Paul, did you live on a pig-breeding smallholding, with your future wife? I came to visit you and you showed me around where the pigs breed.' 'That's right,' Paul said. 'Paul Whitaker!' I answered. 'That's me, John,' he replied.

I felt much better, especially as the Paul Whitaker I knew was a bit younger than me, and was not only a good footballer, but a good friend.

As a footballer, Paul represented the British Army XI, and after a mix-up with signing-on forms, he eventually played for Basingstoke at the Camrose ground, one of the clubs I played for all those years ago.

Even after one hour on the phone, I forgot to ask Paul when they moved to Australia, where in Australia they live, and if he had been able to get involved with football when he settled in his new area.

When you receive a call from an old footballing friend and you chat, you are thinking, maybe we could get together for a few days and catch up on all the years since you have seen him, unless you find he is living in Australia with a family. You then say that you will keep in touch by phone. How amazing, thousands of miles away, yet you get to talk to family or friends within a few minutes of dialling them!

Glen Burnett

I bumped into an old friend today, well, sorry Glen, not as old as me. I went to watch my old club Winchester play Weymouth in a pre-season friendly, which was a very good performance. I was keen to see how well they could do against a side like Weymouth, and who did I meet, but my friend Glen.

There was a group of us talking about the game, and football in general, and Glen's ideas were knowledgeable. Glen only finished managing a club, which I had managed, a few seasons ago, and took them to promotion status after a first class season. I had congratulated him on his achievement, only to hear their promotion had been turned down due to internal problems, which had nothing to do with Glen. We talked about what had happened and what a shock it was for him, but listening to him, he was still upbeat, which is typical of Glen.

At the end of the game, in which Winchester had once again done very well, we had a drink and I asked Glen about his near future in football. The shrug of shoulders said it all. Now, if you are out there and looking for a very good manager, then take it from me, Glen Burnett is your man.

Steve Coppell (Army)

Tranmere Rovers asked the Army Sports Board if they could use their facilities, as they were due to play Aldershot and Reading, both away. The Army gave permission, and they had asked if we had any players who would like to train with Tranmere during their four-day stay. I was lucky to train with them. Johnny King and the ex-Liverpool player, Ron Yeats, were in charge and I really enjoyed the morning session.

After a light lunch, it was back out for some fitness, but Johnny King was called away for a phone call. On his return, he blew his whistle and called everyone in. We stood and wondered. He then called Steve Coppell out and said to the boys, 'Say your cheerios to Steve, because we have accepted Manchester United's offer of £30,000, and Steve is now a Manchester United player, after his medical.'

All the lads clapped and said their goodbyes, and I got to say, 'Well done.' Steve left for Old Trafford and the rest is history.

Mark Falco, Spurs and Millwall

Mark Falco, the centre forward who played at the highest club level for Tottenham Hotspur, Glasgow Rangers and Millwall ended his career playing for Worthing at Woodside Road in Sussex.

Beau Reynolds approached me after training one Thursday evening to discuss the possibility of signing a centre forward who had lots of experience and was willing to join us. Gerry Armstrong was manager at the time, and he said, 'Have a word with Robbo and see what he thinks.'

My answer was yes as we had Richard Tiltman playing up top and Mark would be a very good asset for the team, as Richard had no problem playing wide on the left for us, and there. Our chairman would arrange a meeting with Mark and I agreed to join them.

A couple of days later we set off to meet Mark at Langans Restaurant in Stratton Street off Piccadilly, which at the time, to me, was just a place to have lunch in London. How wrong was I? After we arrived and parked the car, we walked to the entrance, and as we went to enter, the door opened and the very smart doorman said, 'Welcome, Mr Reynolds. Your table is ready and your guest Mr Falco has arrived.'

'Thank you, Michael,' said Beau and walked us over to our table, or should I say his table? And then I realised, this wasn't just a restaurant in London, this was a very upmarket place to eat; you also had a table with your name on it.

As we introduced ourselves and sat down, Beau asked us what we would like for lunch. The waiter came back with a bottle of wine and three wine glasses. I explained my reason for not drinking as did Mark, that we were driving home, so the waiter left the wine and brought Mark and me soft drinks.

We started chatting about the restaurant, and Beau explained that you hire a table 48 hours in advance for a certain day and time, which is guaranteed when you arrive. Anyway, back to football. Beau realised that if Mark agreed to sign, knowing the distance from where Mark lived to Woodside Road, then his wages would also include an allowance to cover his travelling. Without any comeback, Mark leant over and shook Beau's hand in agreement and signed, then shook my hand. 'Excellent!' was my reply.

We chatted while eating our lunch, which was excellent. An agreement was made between Mark, Beau and myself that, if for any reason Mark could not make training, then as long as his fitness didn't suffer, we would accept his reasons.

As coach at the time of Mark's signing for Worthing I had no doubt he was going to improve our team, and later when I was manager Mark proved to be a first-class introduction. Both home, away and in training, Mark, or Bilko his nickname, showed us his love for football and his club, because of his attitude, ability, strength and commitment. I remember Gerry Armstrong telling me how good a signing Mark was, while adding, 'You cannot beat experience.' How right he was. Thank you, Mark!

Richie Damerell

1971, what a good year for my old club, Waterlooville! That was the year they signed a goalkeeper at Jubilee Road called Richie Damerell, and what a very good signing he turned out to be.

As a goalkeeper, he was first-class, and as a man, Richie was a quiet and unassuming gentleman, and from then until today we are still good friends.

Richie played quite a few seasons at Jubilee Road, and was still first choice when I left the club to sign for St Johnstone FC. I have programmes which show that Richie was still first team keeper at the start of the 1977 season: Mr Reliable.

His work was with the Gas Board, and he later became a tutor-cum-teacher at Highbury College, whose students were hoping to gain certificates as 'Gas Safe' engineers, which were then known as 'Corgi' qualified. I attended one of the courses, for which Mr Damerell was the tutor, and thankfully qualified. Richie and Beverley, his wife, live no more than a ten-minute walk from Ann and me and we seem to bump into them on shopping days. Richie pushes a trolley; that's just so that he doesn't drop any eggs, bottles, etc., being a very recognisable goalkeeper in our area.

From Waterlooville, Richie, after many loyal seasons, signed for another of my old clubs, Gosport Borough FC, keeping as many clean sheets as he could, and when he finished, he rounded up a few old players and played in the senior Sunday league in the area, showing his love for football.

A very, very good goalkeeper, a very good friend; and not too bad a tutor! Take care both of you, see you at the checkout!

Roy Beazley, MBE

Yes, Roy Beazley MBE was a big believer in working for various charities to help those who needed help. I was fortunate to play for the ex-Saints, although I never played for Southampton, and that was the main reason I met Roy and worked with him for a while. Another true gentleman, who always thought of others before himself. Whenever I had time to spare and was in Southampton for work or football, I would call and see Roy and his wife for a cup of tea and was always made welcome. My only disappointment was that I never met Paul, Roy's son, who worked alongside Roy at the very successful Academy at Southampton.

My work with Roy was as a coach to the Hampshire Youth FC in the West Counties Championship. Roy was the Manager and Steve Beaney Assistant Manager, neither of whom is with us any longer. Just to work with Roy and Steve was a pleasure, because we loved our football and tried to pass that love on to the young boys we worked with. Thank you Roy, it was my pleasure to work with you.

Hughie has been a friend of mine for quite a few years. He was a civil servant after serving time in the Royal Navy. He settled very near to me and we still get together for football matches. His family is from Manchester and he is a staunch supporter of Man City. Other than the United supporters, most of us enjoy watching City play when on TV. I don't do social media, but my wife Ann does, and Hughie often tells her where he is in the world, either working or enjoying a break.

Hughie was a good footballer while in the Navy, and was with a couple of local teams when he left, but his job was very demanding. He offered to join me and help with the training, etc., wherever I was managing and he proved to be a great help. Early on in our friendship Hughie took me to meet his family, and while we were in Manchester we went to Denis Irwin's testimonial match at Old Trafford. Hughie wasn't a fan, as you can imagine, being a City fan, although he knew and admired good footballers, and Denis Irwin was in that category, plus it was my first visit to Old Trafford.

Thanks, mate. We still get together for games, that's what friends do.

Mark Clothier

Mark played for Hampshire Youth when I was their coach and was working with Roy Beazley. At 17 he proved to be a very good footballer and a good lad all round. Mark could have played almost anywhere in the team, but I always saw him as a midfield attacking player who could set up goal chances for his team mates, and find the back of the net when needed.

I remember watching Mark at other clubs and thought he would be right for us when I managed Alton Town for the second spell. I asked Mark to join us at Alton, and to me, it was the icing on the cake. He was terrific playing just off the front two, and we went on to win the league in 2000-01.

I also remember my 50th birthday. We invited Mark and his then girlfriend Nikki over to help us celebrate my ageing birthday. They arrived with an excellent birthday cake, which she had made in Sunderland colours, something we won't ever forget.

Mark has an unassuming respect for friends, but will make his point if it differs from yours, something I respect very much.

Recently we received an invitation to Mark and Nikki's wedding in 2019, and while they have been together for many years, and have their own home, they have taken time to prepare themselves for a happy and legal time together.

When I managed Blackfield and Langley I would have loved to have signed Mark, but he was settled with his club, Gosport, and stayed loyal to them at the time. That is Mark who, by the way, is also a very good golfer, but that is only when he plays against the old man; that's me, of course. Thank you Mark and Nikki, together you are a perfect couple, and very good friends.

Wayne Shaw and Mark Cole, Two Goalkeepers
Two very good goalkeepers and two very good friends.

Mark, for a keeper, was smaller than you would expect, but when he put that number 1 shirt on, and the referee blew his whistle to start the game, Mark became an extra player, voicing his information to team mates non-stop for 90 minutes, and given his agility in the area, so quick to react when required. Mark remains in sport helping to run Romsey Golf Club, and as in football, is a very nice guy. Thank you, Mark.

Wayne Shaw is very well known in football, also making and serving ice cream at his family's shop-cum-café in West Wellow in the New Forest, where my wife Ann and I would call in when we were down that way. Wayne, as a goalkeeper, was a big forceful character, who would let his opponents know early on in a game that it was his area in front of goal. Wayne's experience in football has kept him in the game with many clubs, one being Southampton, and another Reading, then with one of my old clubs, Totton, as Commercial Manager. Wayne is a very likeable chap, who knows his stuff when it comes to football, but as a goalkeeper he could be frightening to the opposition.

Ecko Elliot, Blackfield and Langley

While working as Manager at Blackfield and Langley, I was introduced to a player whom the Director of Football, Sam Davies, had signed to help us out up front. My information from Sam was that Ecko could play anywhere up top, wide or also in midfield. At training on Thursday evening, I could see that Ecko was a good player with the ball, and when we did some sprinting he was off his mark quicker than most, so this new signing looked very good. As we had played well on the previous Saturday away from home, I discussed the starting line-up with Chris Farrell, and we both agreed to keep the same team, which had gained all three points away from home in our last game. We also agreed that we would give Ecko a good run out for 15 minutes, towards the end of full time.

The match kicked off as normal and within a few minutes I could see Sam walking very quickly from his seat in the stand, where he always watched the game, towards the home bench. When Sam arrived there his only words were, 'John, I want a word.' I turned to Chris saying, 'Take over, mate, until I see what Sam wants.' I stepped out of the technical area and walked away from everyone within hearing distance. Well, I cannot repeat it in print, but I was asked for whom I had named Ecko as a substitute; he should be starting given his ability, or words to that effect. I explained that after our win away from home I felt it was a correct decision that I should not change the starting eleven, as I had only seen Ecko in training and had respected his, that is Sam's, decision to bring Ecko to the club. His answer to me was, 'You should be playing your best eleven from the start,' with a few expletives thrown in. As we were winning at half-time I sent the starting eleven out for the second half, while telling Ecko, 'If we look like keeping the lead, I will give you the last 20 minutes, so be ready.'

I was keen to see Ecko show me his ability, so with 20 minutes to go I sent him on at wide right and it proved just how versatile and good he was, as he terrorised the left back every time he got the ball. I still feel I did the right thing. However, I knew and understood why Sam was upset that I had not started Ecko, and prepared myself for another telling-off in the changing room or the bar. But Sam called me out, shook my hand and said he understood my reasons. I, in turn said, 'Thank you for signing Ecko.'

Paul Kelly, Chairman of Portchester FC

Paul is another chairman of a football club, yet a club I've never managed or played for. Like most non-League clubs they would not survive without people like Paul at Portchester, making sure on match days that every supporter, both home and away, is made welcome.

Prior to becoming involved in non-League football, I know he was involved at my club Sunderland working for the club alongside their manager at the time.

Paul's playing career was cut short at the early age of 19 due to a severe leg break, which virtually stopped him from carrying on as a player in the game he loved. Watching football is not the same as playing the game, but that was all he could do. Yet, as time went by, Paul showed his love for the game by becoming chairman of his non-League club, supporting it financially, and making sure that the supporters, both home or away, had the facilities required to make their day enjoyable, apart from the result, that is.

Of the chairmen I have worked for, rarely do you find one whose love of the game is much greater than when they give their hard-earned money to keep their clubs afloat year in and year out, but do they get the thanks they deserve? From my experience they should support players and staff and should give their all to bring success to their club: that is a chairman's reward. Well done Paul Kelly!

Micky Mister

Micky and I go back a long way as friends, when we both served in the Army. Football brought us together as mates, with Micky being a very good centre half and me being a centre forward. We always had our football to talk about.

Like myself Micky played for the Army side, and what was known as the Corps side for the Royal Corps of Transport. Good times! When we lost our goalkeeper, Chad Gibbons, who died after leaving the Army, I received a call from Micky about Chad's funeral, which was to be held just inside the Welsh border. He said he would drive down to my place in Hampshire and pick me up for the drive to Chad's funeral. By the way, Micky lived in Suffolk, but that was the kind of friend he was.

Prior to the funeral, Micky and I had kept in touch by telephone, and it was a shame we had to get together for a mate's funeral. Also, when I have been trying to locate some of the records for the period when we were quite successful in the Army, Micky gave me the phone number of Billy Thompson, who looks after the sporting and other records going back many years. I phoned Billy and met up with him at Aldershot so he could show me the football records of my time in the Army. Thanks again, Micky and thank you Billy Thompson.

John Kill and Kim Manns

John and Kim are two very good friends, and two very good footballers, both Waterlooville players. John was a central defender and Kim played on the left wing, but the shame of it is, they both passed away when they were young, fit lads, married and settled, and looking forward to seeing what the rest of their lives would bring, Kim with his wife Steph, and John with his, Glynis. John's problem came much earlier than Kim's, and we all at Waterlooville wondered why it is always the good people whom we lose before they have time to live their lives? Football had a part to play in John's passing away. RIP John, my friend.

Kim passed away after suffering the awful motor neurone disease. I had a chance to visit him at his home in Kimbolton Road in Portsmouth on a few occasions, and on one of my visits I took a child's blackboard and chalk, as talking was not easy for Kim. After I explained why I had brought the implements, we both had a good laugh, and were in stitches at some of the questions I was asking and which Kim was answering by writing with chalk on his blackboard. It was the last time I saw Kim, but we laughed for the whole of my visit. Both John and Kim will never be forgotten, whether talking about football, or just as two friends whose lives were short but filled with everything you wanted a friend to be.

Matty Graham

Matt was a player I met when I took the manager's job at Petersfield. He was one of the many players I felt was playing in a league well below his ability. He read the game well, and for a lad who wasn't the biggest defender in the team, I cannot remember any wide right player or winger get the better of him. His attitude was excellent as a player for 90 minutes plus, and he made a very good leader without the captain's armband.

His job was a teacher in a Portsmouth school, and he asked me if I had a granddaughter called Rose who lived with us. 'Yes,' I said. 'We have a laugh,' he said, 'although sometimes I need to tell her off. Ask her when you get home, Robbo.' When I came in from football one evening and Rose was in, I reminded her that one of her teachers played for me at Petersfield, and she told me how well you both got on. I'm sure she gave you headaches at times, and she said what a good teacher and bloke you are, and I agreed.

We used to discuss the games we played afterwards and I always took on board your comments. Hope you are still enjoying your football as much as I enjoyed watching you, and being your manager.

Thanks Matty, keep my old club Alton Town up there in the league, mate!

Steve Johnson and Graham Rix

Steve and Graham were coach and manager at Portchester. Steve who has his coaching badges, has been a mate of mine for years as we are both Sunderland supporters. We travelled together in 1973 to watch Sunderland play Leeds United at Wembley in the FA Cup Final, and yes, we beat them 1-0 with a goal from Ian Porterfield. What a great day we had. RIP Ian.

Steve was a good footballer. He played at the back, and when coaching put a lot of importance on defending properly.

What do I say about Graham Rix? A great professional at the highest level, who was respected in football. From meeting Graham for the first time, we became friends and remain so to the present. After his illness, I sent my regards through Paul Kelly, his chairman. Graham and Steve did a good job at Portchester, although his illness didn't allow him to carry on. I bump into Steve at games and am looking forward to seeing Graham again soon.

Take care Steve, I know we have been relegated, but I hope you haven't given up on Sunderland.

Jason Scannel

To write about Jason as a player is a manager's dream: an all-round player who would play in goal if you asked him. He played across the back four and was another player who gave it everything for his team mates and club. Jason played for me when I took over from Gerry Armstrong as Manager of Worthing at Woodside Road. His work took Jason to the Honda factory in Swindon where his dad worked. The shame was, his work was vital for the family, especially when his dad had a bad accident, which meant the football had to take a back seat.

Jason was at one stage going out with my daughter Lisa, and at the time they both looked settled. My wife, Ann and I were very pleased with their relationship. However, it didn't work out as Jason became very important as the breadwinner for his family and so broke up with my daughter, and he had to put football at the bottom of his list, knowing his own family came first, and especially Jill, his mum.

Yes, Jason was a big loss to the game he loved, but heknew his place was at home with Jill. I can honestly say Jason was a real man and a loss to football, but a real son and husband to his family and all who know him.

Peter Faulkner

Peter was the man who introduced me to Hampshire and became a friend who was for ever making sure that whatever I needed when I left the Army he was there to help. As Chairman of Waterlooville he loved his football, yet I was to learn that Peter was also a very good cricketer with Hampshire. It was in cricket, when he went abroad with his team mates, that Peter was involved in an accident, in which he lost the lower part of his leg. Yes, he walked with a limp, but the problem for him was not being able to stay in sport, whether it was cricket or football, so Peter being Peter, he decided to join Waterlooville, then sited at the Jubilee Road ground in Waterlooville, as chairman.

This happened long before I was introduced to him, but I was soon to learn of his loyalty, when he invited me to his home in Billet Avenue to meet him and the directors of the club, to discuss the possibility of me signing for the Ville. After approximately 30 minutes of listening to Peter and the eight directors, I was impressed with the direction in which they all wanted to progress the Club. I agreed with what they offered verbally and signed a three-year contract without reading the details, which became the norm for every contract I signed. I just wanted to play at the highest level I could. With that Robin Sparsholt handed me a signing-on fee, then Peter asked where we had decided to live, now that I was leaving the Army. I had been offered a rental place at Basingstoke FC if I signed for the club. Peter then offered me a club house next to the Jubilee Road ground until we could afford a mortgage and our own place. Everyone agreed and I shook everyone's hand saying thank you and my new directors left.

Peter and I then sat down in his lounge, where I met Mrs Faulkner, Sylvia. We had a cup of tea and Peter asked me what I was going to do job-wise. I then explained that I had a spell as an apprentice plumber before leaving home to join the Army. 'Did you enjoy it?' Peter asked. 'Yes,' I said, 'I really enjoyed it.' 'Would you like to carry on learning to be a plumber and heating engineer?' I had chosen to do a few months' course before leaving the Army, which is what they offer you when you have only months to do before you leave. 'I have my building business, so I would take you on when you are qualified.'

'Fine,' I said, 'Where do I need to go to become qualified?' 'Eastleigh College,' Peter said. 'I will hopefully sort something out over the next few days and let you know.' When I got home after the meeting and explained to my wife, Ann, like me she was impressed and happy, so we started to organise things straight away.

In 1974 I left the Army, with the feeling things were going to be fine.

I had signed my contract with Waterlooville, I had a club house to move into with my family, and Peter had organised and paid for, a City and Guilds course at Eastleigh College. I qualified, and during the learning period at the college, Ron Stanton, a director at the club, offered me a labourer's job in his flat-roofing business. Lo and behold I was working with Micky Seymour, who had been released from Southampton and joined Waterlooville as a midfield player. I was to realise what a very good player and person he was, on and off the pitch.

Thanks to Peter I qualified with my City and Guilds in plumbing and heating, and little did I know I was to settle in Hampshire, playing for Waterlooville for six seasons, with a break in 1975-76 when I was loaned to St Johnstone in the Scottish Division. I came back to Waterlooville FC to finish playing for them in 1980. My luck and experience were down to Peter Faulkner, who had not only been my chairman, but also a true friend. Thank you, Peter. RIP my friend.

Ray McKee

Ray McKee is a friend and supporter of football, along with his sons Ian and Ben. Ray is an Alton Town man but he will phone me if he thinks we could meet at a game.

When I managed Alton and won promotion, we were refused because the ground was not up to standard. With that news I decided to take on the Camberley Town job as manager. After the season I was asked to return to Alton Town during the months leading up to the new season, in order that we could carry out the changes needed, in case we won promotion. I turned up to find Ray McKee and other supporters ready and willing to help with the safety precautions needed and alterations to the dressing rooms.

Ray is not just a supporter, as I found during the work we carried out. He was there when needed, and even came to watch us training. We ended up gaining promotion and the ground was rated for the next level. I left at the end of the season and joined Winchester City, and if Alton were not playing, Ray would phone me and turn up to our games. He was also attending Andover Town games when I was there. A true supporter of non-League football and a true friend.

Ian Saunders

When I write about friends I usually tell people involved in football that the reason I don't mention their achievements is because, as with Ian Saunders, Sus to most footballers, he has had so much success in his management and coaching of players that I would need sheets of A4 paper to tell you all of the clubs and players that Ian has improved and taken to promotion. He really is a football must, regarding his knowledge, and his way of explaining to his players, both individually and collectively as a team what both he and they can achieve together.

Ian is a very humble man, very approachable and honest, and he loves his football. At the moment, Ian is managing Portchester with his assistant Micky Catlin. His chairman, Paul Kelly, has chosen very good staff to take care of football on the pitch. Knowing Ian and Micky they will give Paul the success they deserve. Portchester is a well-supported club and I'm sure they will give their followers good, entertaining football and success.

Ian, you are well respected in non-League football, both as a manager and as a man, and to me, as a friend. All the best mate!

Matt Andrews

I'm trying to build some confidence into Matt after, and sometimes during, games. Matt is a good non-League footballer with one problem. He puts pressure on himself prior to games. He is such a good friend and could be an asset to his team if he went out to enjoy the game.

I'm not Gareth Southgate, or one of his coaches, but I feel I can offer players confidence regarding what they should be looking for, both with or without the ball. Recently I watched his team, Winchester City playing at Bashley for a trophy donated by a Bashley supporter. Matt was on the bench for the first half. My advice to him would have been to watch Bashley's central defenders, look for the way they play and notice anything they lack, as a pair, which he knew he could take advantage of, so that when he came on, he could have a word with his two wide players and his midfield suppliers, for his chances on goal. Matt is a good friend and he will take me to and from games. All we, or should I say, I, talk about is the forthcoming

90 minutes. I know he has the ability, I'm just trying to give him advice on how to improve it.

Michael Birmingham

Michael is currently managing Horndean in the Wessex Premier League, finishing in the top six. I'm sure he would be aiming for the top of the league in the coming season. Michael and his brother, Dave, are two good footballers, who find losing very hard to swallow, unless the team they lose to are better in most departments on the day. Michael actually plays the game from the technical area, both individually and collectively, knowing his players inside out, and is very knowledgeable with the information he gives his team. Michael is also a manager who listens when talking football. For me, he is a man who deserves success, given the honesty and effort he puts into everything he does. I get to see his club quite often, as their ground is only a couple of miles from my home. Handy!

Michael has also chosen good staff to surround him, which every manager needs when working for success: Duchy Holland and Jason Mann, two very good assistants, who were both good players in their day and know their football. Michael, I wish you every success for the coming season, 2018/19 and just to tell you, mate, I will be watching.

Don Gowans

Don and I worked together at Eastleigh when the club was in the Jewson Wessex League in the 1990/91 season. Don was the manager and I was the club coach. The ground then was known as 'ten acres'. Working with Don was an absolute pleasure. He knew his stuff when it came to non-League football, and I had been fortunate to gain my coaching badge during my time in the Army. We kept things simple and played to our strengths. Up to 1980, the club was known as Swaythling, playing in the Hampshire League, Division One. The club then took on the name of their town, and ever since has been known as Eastleigh.

I have made a lot of friends because of my work in football, and Don and his wife are two more. I met up with Don's wife on the book launch *Eastleigh FC the Story So Far*, only to find Don had passed away. I gave her a hug and said I hadn't known. Once again the loss of a man who loved his family, his football and friends. Thank you Don, for allowing me to be added to that list, which for me is an honour. RIP my friend!

Goff White

Looking back to my Waterlooville days I got to know Goff White, who like myself was a centre forward and fighting for the number nine shirt in the first team. For two players in our situation you would think there would be animosity between us on football days at the club, but just the opposite. We became good friends and still are to this day. Regarding work and football Goff ended up moving to Tadley for work at Aldermaston, and was very involved with the local council.

Eventually, after playing on the green in Tadley, Goff got the ball rolling (excuse the pun!) and Tadley Calleva were granted a new ground with changing facilities up to a standard such that, if the club won promotion, the ground and facilities would allow them to take that promotion, with the proviso that they would be given time to erect a stand with cover for supporters, both home and away.

Now I have not been to their ground since 2016, but thanks to Goff, Tadley Calleva are now a well-known football club. Well done mate!

Kevin Brewster

What can I say about Kevin? If I was able to get together everyone who has had, and still has the pleasure of knowing him, I would put a bet on that we would all be proud to call him a friend, and those who know him as a footballer would echo those sentiments. He is well-mannered and honest, and a very good non-League player at right back when he puts his Sholing shirt on.

If every team had someone like 'Brewy' playing for them, the left-sided players would have to find something in their locker to get past him with the ball. But don't think mixing it on the physical side would show his weakness. His football brain can handle that, and with his team mates at Sholing, they would soon sort out anyone who thought they could try such antics. Dave Diaper, the manager-cum-chairman, has a very strong, physical footballing side, who would look after Kevin. And you know what they say, beware of the quiet ones. Kevin, I have known you a long time mate, and thank you for being a friend.

Terry Brown and Tony Cox

My mate Terry and I have known each other for some time. 'Tez' and I have never had reason not to be mates, and that is after visits and holidays together with a distance of 350 miles between us. You in County Durham and Ann and me in the county of Hampshire, 'down south' as it is known in 'up north' Durham.

I left the Army in 1974 and you left just after me in 1975. I chased the hope of being a footballer, mate and you joined the police force, serving 25 years.

We met in the Army in 1972 at Aldershot and have kept in touch ever since on a regular basis, as have the girls, Ann and Judy, on social media. Apart from when we have been on other holidays together, Gran Canaria has been the holiday resort we love, having small apartments in Vistaflor and knowing lots of friends who we kept bumping into when we organised our holidays to coincide with theirs. The bad news is that a company has bought the resort and owning an apartment is not allowed: the rules have changed. Still, Terry and Judy, Ann and I have been to the USA, Corfu, and still meet up around cities in England.

One of Terry's and my friends was Tony Cox, another footballer who we served with in the Army. We all loved our football. Mind you, Tony had a short fuse when fouled during a game. Tony preferred a fight to a free kick. He passed away a couple of years ago, when he, Maureen and the boys were living in Sheffield. I drove up for the funeral to see our mate Tony buried, but Terry was unable to attend. 'Coxie', we will never forget you mate.

Since we were young, Terry and I have supported Sunderland, first at Roker Park and now at The Stadium of Light. But the last three seasons have been awful. Since the new Chairman, Mr Short took over, he has disappointed terribly with two relegations. Terry is now watching South Shields, who over the past three seasons have won two promotions and the FA Vase. He and I went to Wembley to support them to a terrific victory. Yes, the players and staff were excellent on the day, but the chairman has transformed South Shields, giving belief to supporters, players and staff.

Tez, mind that fence when you jump over to watch Shields at home! Fancy an ex-copper doing that to save £3.50! Well guys, that's Terry Brown for you, but I wouldn't swap him for anyone. Don't change Tez well, apart from walking around to the turnstiles and paying your entrance fee, mate! See you soon!

Jim Steel, ex Pro

Jim was a typical Scotsman; he didn't mince his words when he discussed football. He doesn't mind throwing in the odd swear word now and then, but Jim was honest when involved in a conversation and still is to this day. I wonder how many of you know that when Southampton beat Manchester United at Wembley in the 1976 FA Cup Final, due to Bobby Stokes, 'Steely' was man of the match. Not many know. Why? Because Jim doesn't say much about it, even when we are discussing football.

Jim had a good career ahead of him in Scotland with Dundee, though he wanted to play for his home club in Edinburgh. A 'jambo' as the Hearts were known, came round to his house to sign Jim, but his dad made him stay with Dundee, as he had shaken hands with Bobby Ancell, Dundee's Manager, so Jim became a Dundee player.

It wasn't long before Jim was wanted by Southampton. Though it was out of his comfort zone, Jim saw it as a step up in the game he'd loved since a boy, and the rest was history.

Jim's career at Southampton as a strong, yet very approachable defender, whose attitude to win became a must, made him a regular choice in the first team. I was fortunate to become a team mate of Jim's in the Southampton ex-professionals, travelling all over Hampshire in charity games, and travelling over to France for an over-40s football competition in which we reached the final, playing a Bayern Munich team.

Peter Osgood was our manager, and we did very well, given that the Germans had two players who were a lot younger than 40. I had heard them discussing their team, and what they were going to do to us in the final. My three years serving in the Army in Germany and playing for a German club meant I had learnt the language quite well and confronted their players about the competition and the rules. Peter confronted their manager but the final went ahead. Having players like Jim, Billy Beaney and Jimmy Case we decided to treat the Germans to a physical encounter, which they did not like at all. We felt that we had been cheated, but still enjoyed our few days abroad.

After stepping down from Southampton first team, Jim was invited across the pond, as they say, to play in the USA for Washington Diplomats, Chicago Sting, and Memphis, finally playing as Captain of Pittsburgh Spirit in a very illustrious, lengthy and successful career, playing alongside Johan Cruyff and Pele, just to mention a few. On coming home he ran a very successful pub in the Cotswolds with his wife, Gillian. My wife and I used to drive up to see them both on Sundays, always enjoying our time with them, and sometimes going up with the lads. Jim became a good friend and finally moved back to Southampton with Gill. We are still good friends, so much so that Jim helped my niece through her finals at Southampton University, studying sports media.

Thanks, mate and a true friend.

Micky Catlin

In my time as a coach and manager at various clubs, I've had Michael as a player and an assistant, yet to date, I have never heard anyone bad mouth him, ever. Had they done that in front of me, or within earshot, I would have asked, 'What gives you the right to talk about my friend like that?' However, the next time will be the first. Michael was very good as a holding player, or a full back, and whether I played him at full back or in the midfield, he would never complain, just on with his strip, then out onto the pitch. He never tried to do something he couldn't do, he kept it simple and did what was asked of him. I used to hear, 'Robbo, Micky Catlin is too nice a guy to step up to coaching and managing.'

'Well,' I used to ask them. 'What do you want from a player, someone who can't be told, and who complains about his team mates, or a player who goes on to the pitch to give 100% to all who are involved with his club, including players and supporters?' I know, because I would ask him to follow me, if and when I changed clubs, as a player and as an assistant.

When I visit clubs to watch a game, I often bump into friends. Michael is now working at Portchester, a good club with Ian Saunders as manager with Michael alongside.

When I signed Michael from Horndean, in 1986, he was 22 years old. In his first season, he won Player of the Year at Petersfield, and we won promotion to the Vauxhall Opel League.

I then went to Sussex for a spell with Southwick, then had a season under my friend John Waugh as his coach at the Walled Meadow, Andover Town. We were a southern league side then and finished a creditable sixth. Michael joined me on loan from Waterlooville at Southwick and Worthing. He then joined me at Gosport as my assistant.

To sum up what Michael had to offer as both a footballer and friend, he was and still is, an honest and reliable man. I hope that the players at each club he has represented take note of the way he conducts himself in life, whatever he does. Thank you, Michael.

Jamie Bray

What can I say about Jamie that has not been said by numerous people who have met and known him? He is full of life, bubbly, and quite a knowledgeable guy in most subjects. Jamie runs his own business and also puts on events, mainly for charities, and all sorts of entertainment get-togethers. And while Jamie and his staff sit happily in his office, at the events I have attended, no stone is left unturned. Jamie also has a lovely lady by his side, Jess, but no matter what you do, the ladies seem to offer ideas in whatever you do, and you think, 'Yes, she is right.' That's Jess, Jamie. Am I right?

Jamie is also a good goalkeeper, and as in his job, he is also very well organised on the football pitch. He is never quiet, whether it is in his office, or on the pitch. The men in his business and his back four on the pitch are told, whether it be a corner, free kick, or the opposition attacking with the ball. The only time and place he is not in charge is at home. His lovely lady Jess wears the hat, and on it is, 'Ask the boss before you do anything.'

Sandy, Steve and Nigel

Sandy Brown, Steve Riley and Nigel Thwaites were servicemen, Sandy an Army man, and Steve and Nigel Navy men. Whether it is football or life in general, discipline is there, whatever they do, and this was evident on the football pitch. These lads represented the Army (Sandy) and the Navy (Steve and Nigel) at the highest level, while serving their country. And I can tell you, these lads could play. Both Steve and Nigel played for me at Worthing when we were very successful, gaining promotion and winning trophies, I also tried to sign Sandy, after watching him play for the Army and clubs. When sweepers were playing just behind a back three, Sandy was class, but could also cover positions in midfield.

Steve Riley was a centre half. Not the tallest, but his timing when challenging for the ball was second to none, and his attitude was always to win, for himself and his team mates. As a lad from the north east, when he moved down to Hampshire, he approached me, asking if I could help him find a club. Having watched Steve play with the Navy, I had no problem saying that I would ring a few clubs and recommend Steve to them. Prior to Steve signing for me at Worthing, he was the talk of the football town wherever he played. As a friend and quality central defender, I took him to Worthing and for Worthing he became a 'seven out of ten' every game. Steve is now retired from football, and now and then Steve and Justine and Ann and I get together for a meal, so the girls can chat about girlie things, and Steve and I chat about Newcastle United, Steve's club and Sunderland AFC, my club. None of us thought Newcastle would be tenth in the Premier League, while we have just been relegated from the Championship, 24th April 2018. It's in my diary!

Nigel Thwaites is another lad from the north east, Middlesbrough to be exact. We are now talking about an attacking player either side, right or left, with pace. Nigel was another representative in the Navy XI. He moved to Cornwall with his wife Karen prior to leaving the Navy. Nigel came to Worthing at Steve's recommendation. It didn't take me long to see the quality he would bring to our side, once again an ex-Navy and combined services player.

Nigel asked me if I would travel to Helston in Cornwall and do some work in a house he and Karen had purchased. Not realising the distance and where I could pick up materials, I said yes, as it was the start of a new life for both of them. What an experience! But considering I had a friend who put himself out to play for me at Worthing (and what a player!), down I went, working from Sunday until Fridays during the closed season, making Saturdays for pre-season friendlies.

When I had finished, Nigel and Karen left their Navy quarters in Hampshire and moved down to their first house. Once settled, Nigel looked to join a club in Cornwall and played for Falmouth Town, then Truro City FC. No doubt he made both clubs a better side.

A couple of weeks ago Ann and I decided to go to Cornwall for four days and while there, we visited the Eden Project, as Ann wanted to do the zip wire run. We decided to contact Nigel and Karen in Heston. We were made so welcome and enjoyed an evening out with them, which made our visit a really enjoyable few days. We left, making sure we would stay in touch and we will.

All I can say is they are three servicemen whose class on a football pitch brought us together, and whose discipline gave me, as a manager, when naming my team, a no brainer when these three were available. Their names were down to start wherever we were fortunate to be involved.

These guys help clubs to win leagues and silverware. What a great sport football is, at all levels, and what pleasure it gives supporters, coaches and managers when you are blessed with players like Sandy, Steve and Nigel. Thank you guys!

Mick Marsh

On Friday 27th April I drove over to Gosport FC to attend a charity match for a 15-year-old young lady, Katie Scannel, who had suffered cancer and passed away two months earlier. The charity was organised in aid of Katie by Mick Marsh and my son Darren, but the shame was that because of the rain the attendance could have been a lot better. Knowing Mick, he could have topped up the takings, because that's the kind of man he is.

We have known each other for years through football. Mick recommended me to take over from him when he was Manager of Gosport Borough FC. He was battling to run his business and manage the club. Today our get-togethers are few and far between, but when we do meet, we enjoy covering the ground we've missed. Mick is a Paulsgrove boy, near Portsmouth, which is supposedly known for its rough and ready folk, but I have met lots of people from there during work as a plumber and heating engineer, and meeting people through football, when my son Darren managed the club for a few seasons. My younger son, Scott, lives there and if their standards match up to Mick Marsh's, then I have no worries. Mick is a listener, a gentleman and a knowledgeable man who sets a very high standard of living. Being a Paulsgrove lad has a lot to do with it.

Guy Butters

Guy Butters, Spurs, Portsmouth, Brighton and Gillingham, and three under-21s England caps, adding up to 672 total games. Now that is a career in football! Yet he never gave anyone the impression he was a Bobby Moore, or Franz Beckenbauer, just Guy Butters.

We met obviously through football at different stages, some after Guy was a coach and as a manager. Bumping into a friend now and then was great, but it was when we worked as scouts that we enjoyed keeping the clubs we worked for aware of players and opponents, often comparing notes while doing our work.

I remember one game in particular, when we phoned each other about where we were going to be the following day, only to find we were both travelling in the same direction, so we decided to travel in one car. When we arrived, while I was there to watch the home team's right back, Guy was reporting on the team due to play, who he was scouting for. Anyway, he did his job and I did mine, and after the game, we decided to go into the bar before driving home. I went to the bar for two soft drinks, and when I returned to the table, Tommy Widdrington was sitting with Guy, the Eastbourne Manager, which was where we were. Tommy was a friend to both Guy and me and asked why we were both at the game together. Our explanation gave us away, but the good thing was that Tommy didn't drop us in it. Thanks Tommy!

A while has passed since we have seen each other, as Guy was offered work at Brighton as a welcoming person at home games. To be honest, they could not have picked a better person and footballer to welcome guests. Good choice Brighton!

Jamie Barron

Jamie is a Southampton lad. We first met at Salisbury FC when Simon Browne and I were asked to form a team from the reserves and youth team to enter the Suburban League. Simon and I realised there would be lots of long away journeys, and it would be physical. As we sat down to discuss the players we would pick, we decided to choose a squad of 16 players each to see how close we were to each other's choices.

Jamie Barron was on both our selections, along with Lewis Benson and Joe Fisher, two midfield players and a strong centre half. After some thinking between us, we had named our squad for this new venture; now we needed a captain and a leader. Well, Jamie was a leader from the dressing rooms, as were Joe and Lewis. There was a big decision to be made, since we knew the three we had selected were all capable, and would gain respect from the rest of the team.

Not too long after our success in the Suburban League and Cup Double, Jamie was looking for a job, and as I had my own plumbing and heating business, I thought, yes, he could work as my apprentice, learn the trades, then take his certificates. I gave him the choice after discussing it with his dad, who rarely missed a game wherever we were playing, and Jamie was on board and proved to be very conscientious in his work and his football. We got on well at work, as we had our love of football to discuss, no matter what level. Surprisingly, we rarely agreed about the teams in the Premier League, as Southampton was Jamie's club and mine was Sunderland.

Jamie had a girlfriend at the time called Stephany, who was training to be a hairdresser. She was very successful at the time, earning more than Jamie, even with his football expenses and his wages from myself, which at times I felt guilty about and more so when they became engaged. But like most couples, the females always manage to teach us males about finance, and they are now married and have a young daughter, Olivia. Jamie is still in football for Winchester City, which I used to manage back in the day, while Steph is bringing up their daughter and hairdressing, when Jamie can baby sit.

To sum up Jamie, football has been a love for as long as he has known Steph his wife, but Steph and Olivia come first. Jamie is a very good lad/man who can be trusted by all, especially his wife and family. I'm sure he takes after his dad, who, together with his mam, played a big part in his growing up, making him the man he is today. We still bump into each other at games and enjoy a chat afterwards, and when he is working in my area, he will always call in for a cuppa.

Thanks for being a friend as well as a footballer, Jamie. All the best to you and your family.

Dean Beale GK

What is there to say about Dean? Just imagine you were 6 feet 3 inches tall, good looking, a male model, a very good goalkeeper, oh, and by the way, the male modelling was with Ann Summers. What was there to dislike about Dean, apart from the modelling for Ann Summers? We were all envious of him, and to sum it up, he was a great guy.

Dean was with me at Worthing in the 95-96 season after we gained promotion to the Isthmian Premier League. I had known Dean through football for a few years when he was with other clubs. He was at Southampton, Sunderland, Basingstoke, Newport IoW, Poole Town then Worthing. After he had served the professional clubs, he started his double glazing company, and to this day he still has a thriving business, though every now and then he drops the odd pane of glass. Not good for a goalkeeper, at the top of a ladder!

We have remained friends, so much so that when we bought our houses at more or less the same time, Dean fitted my double glazed windows and doors, while I installed the plumbing and heating fixtures, which he and Gail, his wife, needed in their new home, and for both of us it was a great deal. That's what friends do, when football brings players together.

Dean and Gail have two sons, Samuel and Harrison. Samuel is a good goalkeeper himself, and I'm sure he could find a club and make the goalkeeper's shirt his own, especially having been at Eastleigh learning his trade with Southampton Academy. Harrison is very much a fisherman, something about which I have not a clue. He is learning about his hobby at Sparsholt College, which can only help when he takes to the rivers, lakes and the seas.

The only part I find difficult to accept is that when you catch a big fish, you take a photo of your catch, then gently put it back in the water. If you think about it, it's similar to being a goalkeeper, like his brother Samuel. Someone shoots, Samuel saves, then throws the ball back onto the pitch, so someone can have another shot.

Kevin Smith, Alton 2010-11

When I took over the job to manage Alton Town in 1998, I accepted the staff who had worked at Alton during the previous season. One person stood out, regarding his knowledge within the club and the players we had to choose from, and that was Kevin Smith, a qualified coach and ex-Army man. We both set targets, and stuck to the plan, bringing in a few new players to get the balance we needed within the squad. Kevin made sure our players knew what we needed, both in ability and discipline, which took a lot of pressure off me as I knew what we were going to do on training nights. Preparation was discussed over the phone, and our Friday evening calls prior to Saturday's match could last 30 minutes or more.

Kevin was the kind of guy who would touch on things we needed to change, if we had injuries, or absentees through illness. We made sure players were aware of our changes within the squad prior to games. Even when we disagreed, Kevin knew the decision was mine, but I always thought deeply about his ideas and reasons for changes. In the 98-99 season we won the league yet did not gain promotion due to the ground not having the necessary facilities. I then made a decision to leave Alton Town while Kevin stayed on and kept the standards up. I joined Camberley for the next season, only to return to Alton and gain promotion.

Tony and Connor Cocklin

I often wonder why so many fathers see their sons as future footballers playing in the Champions or Premier Leagues, but they don't make it to or near the top. Hundreds, thousands maybe. However, a good friend of mine is a father to a son, Connor, who has played for me, yet never once when we are together watching, or over the phone, does he put Connor on a pedestal, saying he is better than anyone on the pitch. He can be critical of Connor, or give a 'Well done Connor.'

I actually rate Connor as a very good defender, as he is tall and fit, with a good pace, and who reads the game very well when defending or covering his team mates. I do feel he can do better when he goes up for corners and free kicks, and Tony, his dad, would sometimes agree. Now Tony obviously played at a good non-League level and does enjoy seeing his son play well. I imagine Tony being a tough midfield holding player, or a strong front runner, putting his head where people won't put their feet.

We have kept in touch regarding the fixtures Connor plays, even though we are some 50 miles apart, and Tony knows I have recommended Connor to clubs and managers, yet he is the first to criticise Connor to me, if he feels his son hasn't done well for his team.

I've learned from Tony how not to put pressure on Connor, just by being at every game he can. I realise that as a dad he can't always be at every game Connor plays in, but what he does do, is to allow his son to give him his version of the match. Without praise or criticism, he just listens to his son. I find myself very comfortable when Tony and I get together to watch Connor. He knows his football and he knows his son. First, enjoyment, then a win, is all he asks. He knows we can't all be Bobby Moore or Rio Ferdinand, at the back. Tony is a good friend and a very good dad. Cheers Tony!

Steve and Wendy Cowley

Steve is an ex-serviceman from Leicester, and is a true supporter of the club, so much so my wife Ann and I are waiting for him and Wendy to come down to stay with us for as long as they want so that Steve can go to St Mary's to watch Southampton play Leicester. I went to St Mary's ticket office recently and bought two tickets for us in the Leicester end. For Steve I did the right thing. However, if Saints score first, I must remember not to cheer!

Steve and Wendy met Ann and me in Gran Canaria, Maspalomas to be exact, while on holiday, and we arranged to meet again, spending time together, soon becoming friends, staying in touch by phone. They do quite a lot of travelling, showing their interest in 'northern soul', wherever it's on in England and they are able to go, sometimes combining it with football. If the venue is near to a team Leicester are playing, Steve will be there, hence their games at St Mary's. Steve left the stadium last time very happy, with Leicester winning 2-1, Harry Maguire scoring the winner. He is a player I recognise as a very good centre half, after watching his performance for England in the World Cup.

Steve was, himself, a very good centre half, playing for Coalville and being invited to Leicester in his younger days.

The Boys from City (plumbing that is)

Chris, Joe and Sid, three friends who I see quite often, are guys who work at City Plumbing. Chris Summers, the manager, is a big supporter of Middlesbrough, Joe McNeill follows Everton, and Sid Law is a keen supporter of Portsmouth. Sid lives in Portsmouth, which allows him easy access to Fratton Park, while Joe and Chris work on Saturdays from 7.30 am until 12 pm, meaning that they can only watch Everton and Middlesbrough when they are down south. Then, you can bet they will be there to cheer their teams on.

Now that I am retired, I call in and see them as often as I can and make them a cup of tea or coffee, as Chris is a coffee man. When I was working as a plumber and heating engineer, they were my only supplier of the fixtures I needed for my work, and if what I needed was out of stock, then they would source it for me and have it delivered to where I was working. In the meantime, football was our topic of interest, and with me supporting Sunderland, I was the butt of the jokes. Talking about jokes, Joe was always ready with jokes we had never heard. He was so good at delivering jokes, he would keep us laughing while we were trying to drink our tea, or coffee. When I left, with exactly what I wanted for my day's work, I always left laughing, thinking Joe could be on the television, as his talent as a comedian was first class. Mind you, being a Scouser helped. You don't see many miserable people from Liverpool, unless they have just lost to the Kopites.

As for Joe's workmates, both Chris and Sid had probably heard Joe's funnies before, but still laughed, which would make him ideal to stand on a stage and entertain a packed audience with his never-ending quips and funny stories. Thanks, Joe, for always making me happy while on my way to work, and to Chris and Sid, who when Joe is on form, always take a back seat while their workmate is in the spotlight. There is no jealousy; like me they just enjoy it. Three friends who while they are working allow me to make the drinks and chat, not always about football or plumbing materials. It is a pleasure to spend time with the boys from City. Thank you, Chris, Joe and Sid. Long may it continue!

Simon Browne

I first met Simon when I joined Salisbury in 2005. He was a very good defender with the first team. During my first few months running the youth and reserves Nick Holmes realised I needed help at times, and he asked Simon to work with me on training evenings and Saturday home games, as Simon lived in Weymouth. We worked together, and within a couple of weeks it worked well. We both had enough humour and football experience to encourage the players to listen and put things into practice, which led to the amazing season we had in the Suburban League, being unbeaten in the League, and going on to win the Surburban Cup Trophy at Imber Court at the end of a tremendous run of some 32 league games, winning 31 and drawing one, then winning the cup after six unbeaten rounds.

Yes, you have to have players who are good enough to be asked to make changes each week, what with injuries, and losing players to the first team squad, but the season showed how they reacted to Simon and me. When Simon and I left the club, Simon became Manager at Hamworthy near Poole, under the very-respected Steve Harvey their chairman. Simon did a very good job, taking over from Phil Simkin who had won the Dorset Senior Cup.

Simon's aim was to assess his first team squad, reserves and younger players, then prepare them for the road ahead. I managed to get down for a few training sessions and games at Simon's request, and thoroughly enjoyed helping out. Simon served the club until 2013, and to this day I stay in contact with my friends Simon and Steve. That's football!

Alan Mullery 1990

If you receive a call from someone who has played for Spurs and England asking you to work alongside him as a coach to the team he has taken over as manager, then you don't need to ask him any questions. You just say yes, and thank you, when do I start?

The club was Southwick, in the Isthmian League in 1990. I knew I was about to learn more about football from an England player.

Alan was a great man to work with. He didn't need to shout and scream at the players, yet when he addressed the lads in his pre-match talk, and before a training evening, they all listened, as I did. Very rarely did any of the players question him, even though he offered them the opportunity.

He and I had chatted about where we needed to be better, and he put a lot of emphasis on keeping our discipline and sticking to what we had talked about and practised in training. Not once did he demand anything which he knew our players had not done in training, yet building their confidence for match days was his preparation chat to each individual. Alan would be out on the pitch during the pre-match warm-up, telling the players how important they were to the team, and what we were collectively as a team; something I picked up on for coaching and managing.

As a man, there was never any, 'Do you realise I played for Spurs and England?' Alan was a gentleman and became a good friend. We have met at football functions over the years, and Alan Mullery is still the same humble man I was lucky to work with.

Craig Davis

Craig started his football career at Cardiff FC and was there as a young player for three years. However, Craig left Cardiff when they were relegated due to finance. At 20 years old he was sold to Salisbury FC after a short stay at Bashley, for an amount Bashley couldn't refuse. Craig was then sold on to Fleet Town FC as a player, and a very good player, who could cover most positions in midfield or at the back. His stay at Fleet as a player was a very successful one, and eventually he took over as player-manager; a role that suited him and Fleet Town very well.

Although Craig and I met at football matches, our respect for each other as friends didn't take long to show itself when he asked me to join him while Fleet were training, just to join in and get to know the players, and cast an eye on what I thought would improve results. I trained and watched their games with pleasure, enjoying sharing ideas with Craig, even when we disagreed. That for me was respect and it worked both ways. Craig has since taken over at Winchester City, and I'm sure he will bring stability and success. Why? Because his knowledge and hard work will give him the success he deserves. In any sport, if you manage a team, you have different players with different personalities, and you must ask things you want, before the kick-off. Craig does just that; he asks but does not demand. As a player-manager you could leave yourself wide open to criticism during the game at half time, or when the final whistle is blown. However, Craig's temperament and personal criticism means he will apologise for any mistake that was costly to his team, not that he needs to but he will. Honesty is paramount when discussing the game with his players and staff.

Yes, we are friends, and very good friends, and while Craig has asked me to help him occasionally, I have learned an awful lot from him, and am very grateful to have him as a friend.

Jim Storrie, Waterlooville and St Johnstone

While playing for Waterlooville under manager Jim Storrie, I found his methods of systems played were very precise and well thought-out prior to games, both home and away. I, as well as our players, understood the minor details as Jim was a top professional, which I saw when he took me on loan from Waterlooville to St Johnstone. The coaching and fitness were, to Jim, the most vital part of his work as a manager. We were allowed a laugh during training, both at Waterlooville and St Johnstone, but when it came to the jobs we had as individuals, he would make you aware that not carrying out your jobs would not be accepted, which meant you would be sitting and watching the game, as opposed to playing in the game.

Jim passed away a few years ago now, but he changed my life in many ways both at Waterlooville and St Johnstone. Whereas a thank you isn't enough, I adopted his ideas and work ethic which played a big part in my playing, coaching and managing. Thank you, Jim.

Nick Holmes, Southampton and Salisbury

Nick invited me down to Salisbury asking me to run the Reserves and the Youth teams. This was fine for me, although the travelling on the A36 could sometimes be a pain. Nick explained that a mix of reserve and youth team players would be eligible to enter the Suburban League, which he thought would be a good league for them to complete in. His main job was the first team squad, with Barry Blankley as assistant, and a very experienced Tommy Widdrington as his coach. Given the time Nick spent with the first team squad, he always took time out when training to wander over to us and make sure the players were listening and doing what I asked and Simon Browne, my assistant, demanded.

After a training session we would have a meeting to discuss how we felt things were going. Nick also made sure we connected with our players as to social and any family problems. I worked at Salisbury for four seasons under Nick and can honestly say I enjoyed every minute, and to this day, if I travel to the Ray Mac Stadium, Nick always takes time after the game to have a chat. An excellent manager and a true friend and gentleman!

John Waugh and Dave Green

John was a manager I played for and worked under, and Dave Green was a goalkeeper who also worked alongside me at a few clubs, both friends who loved the game and were genuinely sensible when it came to football.
John was very experienced, having managed Workington Town before moving south. John also managed in the USA and on his return took the manager's job at Waterlooville, and did a very good job, but his health became the reason to take up a supporter's role, watching, only to find that cricket became the sport for him.

Dave, on the other hand, stayed loyal to football, working with me at Alton Town. An excellent gardener, he still to this day works at Winchester City, doing jobs at the ground.

It's now 2018 and the three of us get together each Friday morning to play golf at Avington golf course. A friend, Brian, makes the foursome, with our football and golf spanning some 20 plus years, as friends through football.

Sam Davies and Owen Lightfoot

Two guys who are the reason why Blackfield and Langley is such a well-run club are Sam Davies and Owen Lightfoot. Sam is the Director of Football and Owen is the Chairman, both putting the club first on and off the pitch.

Sam is very much hands-on regarding the players coming into the club and leaving, and with all of the movement, Sam would talk it over with the manager. When Sam came over to ask me if I would be the manager, he came with Kevin Gibbons, a player who Sam had brought to the club to wear the number 9 shirt. Kevin, an ex-professional with Southampton, proved to be the best signing Sam made when recruiting players, and the first name on the team sheet for me. Also, Sam would take me to meet players I wanted to sign. We went to sign Andy Forbes, a goal scorer and Charlie Knight, a left-sided midfield player. Andy was up near Reading and Charlie in Stockbridge. No one could have tried harder than Sam to sign the two players he knew nothing about.

Now and then Sam would phone me for a chat over lunch. The venue was two miles from his offices, but for me it was a 60-mile return trip. Still, the food was good at the garden centre. That was Sam, but when you worked for him and got to know him, he was, and still is, an excellent director of football, and more to the point, a very good friend. I still travel to Blackfield and Langley matches, and Sam Davies and Owen Lightfoot are their best supporters, given what they do for the club. Owen is a behind-the-scenes worker. If someone was missing from the club staff for whatever reason, you would find Own standing in.

These two friends are the reason why the club is always looking for promotion.

However, in non-League football no one on the staff who does the behind-the-scenes work gets paid. But for people like Sam and Owen, their club comes first and, trust me, I have met plenty of Sams and Owens who support their club no matter what, without looking for financial rewards. It's just a shame that players don't have the same attitude as they have, especially as players love their 90 minutes of football.

Sam genuinely loves to get involved and help out, no matter what. Having been involved with numerous non-League clubs and players, who are well looked after, both on and off the pitch, I see Sam is the perfect director of football, a main reason why Blackfield and Langley are always battling for promotion and cups. For what he does for the club, he alone deserves all of the success which comes his way.

Chris Farrell

I met Chris when I took over the Manager's job at Blackfield and Langley. Sam Davies, the Chairman, offered me the job. Sam introduced me to Chris Farrell, my number two and coach. Chris had been assistant to managers before I took over in 2014. He came from Cannock in Staffordshire, playing local football and working as a coal miner for 17 years until, like many mines, his was closed. Chris decided to move south, looking for work in and around the Bournemouth area, and got himself a job and a club. He joined Hamworthy United, where he spent six seasons. From there he spent a short time at Bournemouth Poppies before moving to Blackfield and Langley as assistant to Ashley Vickers, another good friend of mine, thanks to football.

They were very successful. Glen Burnett, another good friend, took over as manager from Ashley while Chris stayed with Blackfield and worked alongside Glen. Success followed them. Glen stepped down and I was offered the job in 2014, with Chris staying on as my assistant, which turned out to be a big help for me. I actually joined the club with eight games left from the previous season. Chris was a massive help, knowing the players and the club inside out. He knew the players' attitudes and their capabilities on the pitch, which gave me the players we needed to keep, and those we needed to replace, which is the worst part of a manager's job.

The main thing that I liked about Chris was that he had his own opinion on matters regarding football, players and their attitudes. No matter what we discussed together, Chris would not change his mind. This I respected, given that I was starting my first full season with Blackfield, while Chris was starting his eighth. Enough said! You need someone alongside you who is going to attend all training nights, games and meetings when you are signing new players.

Chris was always there, and early enough for us to prepare our sessions for training and matches. When we disagreed with each other he knew it was my decision, but when the outcome showed he was right, he let me know. Chris is still a close friend, and we stay in touch.

Chris's claim to fame was that he played in the same team as Stan Collymore, but to his credit he doesn't brag about it. I wonder if Stan says he played alongside Chris Farrell? Who knows? Take care mate!

Dave Leworthy Trial 1984, Harrow-on-the-Hill

While I was serving as coach to Richie Reynolds at Fareham, things were going OK, but we were still looking to strengthen our squad. Then, out of the blue, there was talk in the area that Dave Leworthy had been released from Portsmouth. Knowing Dave as a footballer and friend, I was so disappointed for him, as he was a person with a great character, who I felt was destined for top flight soccer, which he showed us in the games he played. Dave was far too good for non-League football in my opinion.

One evening when watching Match of the Day and aware of the players and teams I was watching, I decided to phone the then Chairman of Tottenham Hotspur, Bill Nicholson, who wasn't so much a friend, more of an acquaintance, as he came from the same area as me, in the north east. On the Monday I phoned and asked if I could speak to Mr Nicholson. The receptionist asked my name, and the next voice, that of Bill Nicholson said, 'Hello, John, how are things with you and what do you want?'

I then explained about the footballer who had just left Portsmouth and who I felt was worth a trial at the highest level. Bill Nicholson explained that they were holding a friendly at Harrow-on-the-Hill the following week and he would mention it to Peter Shreeves, the Manager, to get the OK, and, either way, he would get back to me. I also knew Mike Varney, the physio to the first team, as he had been physio to the Army team prior to leaving to join Spurs. I gave Bill Nicholson my home number and asked him to phone me, because if I didn't get Dave a trial I was the only person at my end who knew. I received a call the following day which was a yes from the manager, Peter Shreeves, kick-off at 7.45 pm. Brilliant!

Dave's dad, brother Perry, myself and Dave travelled up to Harrow, getting to the ground in plenty of time, so Dave and I went to the dressing rooms hoping to find Peter Shreeves to introduce Dave to him. Within five minutes Peter Shreeves came out from the home dressing room and realised Dave was a player as he was standing in his track suit with his bag.

'You must be Dave Leworthy and you are John.'

He then said, 'In the home dressing room I'm starting you up top, and John, can you come to the Manager's office, and I will tell you how I feel about Dave?'

Out came the teams, and the game was under way. Forty-five minutes later, I knew the outcome, as I walked to the manager's office. Dave was excellent, scoring on three occasions and looking the class player and person he is. The door was open as I knocked. Dave's dad had followed me there. Peter Shreeves and Dave were in the office as we walked in; Peter was offering Dave a two-year contract with an apartment. Dave told me the contract was fine, and as Dave's dad and I walked out Peter Shreeves thanked me for recommending Dave to the club. After he had signed and witnessed his new contract with the club secretary Dave went into the dressing room to get changed. We waited, overlooking the second half. We both told Dave that he had been excellent in the first half.

'Thanks,' Dave said. 'I felt comfortable out there, and the team mates made it so easy for me.' Typical of Dave!

We went back to where Perry was watching the game and the expression on his face told us he knew how well his younger brother had done. When we broke the news, Perry was chuffed to bits. I can tell you, the ride back home to Pompey was much better than the nervous ride up. Well done Dave!

When I arrived home that evening I was more pleased than anyone. Dave Leworthy was now a Tottenham footballer with a contract, an apartment and a future on the big stages in the First Division. The next day I picked up the phone and thanked Bill Nicholson, and asked him to pass my thanks on to Peter Shreeves. He then told me of the discussion he had had with the manager, who had mentioned

Dave's 45 minutes as being excellent and how fortunate he felt that Dave had signed his contract.

Although I was busy in football myself, I kept in touch with Dave, and every month received photographs and letters about what Dave was doing, such as getting into the first team squad and then getting his minutes on the pitch.

Knowing Dave, the way I do, the things he needed for top-flight football he had in abundance. First of all, he had the ability, both on and off the pitch, to work hard, and be honest within himself if he wasn't yet in the starting XI, and would take on board all the advice given him by the manager and down through the squad of players. It didn't take long for the players to give him a nickname, 'Burger'. I didn't ask why, but had a good idea! One thing he did, above all, that is needed at a top club in the top division was he kept himself fit. It wasn't long before he was a starter and a goal scorer for Spurs and kept his shirt. The rest is history.

When I was managing Worthing in the early 1990s I was given the opportunity to sign a centre forward who still had a couple of years left in him, and would pass his experience on to the team: Mark Falco, who my Chairman and I signed in Langans Restaurant. When you sign a player of Mark's ability and experience the contract is sorted in 15 minutes, then over lunch you start talking about football careers. I got round to telling Mark about my connection with his club through Bill Nicholson, and asked if he had played alongside Dave Leworthy.

'You mean "Burger"?' he replied, and went on to sing Dave's praises. I jumped in and said, 'Bilco,' and Mark said, 'Did you get that from "Burger"?' 'Correct,' I said. 'We got on well on and off the pitch, and what a good player he was.'

So was Bilco when he played for us at Worthing. He scored goals, led the line and showed us what a very good signing he was. Coincidence! Just like Dave at Tottenham.

Bobby Gill

I first met Bobby when he was playing at centre half for Guildford City on their pitch. He was a very difficult player to get past, so much so that Waterlooville signed him from Guildford and we ended up together at Jubilee Road in the same team. We soon became pals and to this day we have remained good friends, with Ann and me staying over at their home in Stubbington after an evening out for a meal. As we got older, Bob moved clubs while still playing, as did I, when returning from playing in Scotland. When we finished playing, we both stayed in touch. Golf is our game now, and while we are average, we still enjoy 18 holes, no matter who comes out on top. Take care Bob and Jenny.

Jimmy Case

I met Jimmy through football and, obviously, in the early days of getting together our chats were about the clubs Jimmy had played for and the trophies he had won. Yet neither Jimmy nor all of the friends whose names everyone knows in football ever bragged about their achievements during playing, and Jimmy's were many.

He took me to Anfield on a couple of occasions, and after the game we went into the players' lounge to meet the players. On one occasion Michael Owen came in to find me talking to his dad. I could tell how proud he was of his son; however when Michael joined us, his dad reminded his son of both the good and not so good about his game against Arsenal. Typical Scouser, said it as it was!

When playing in charity matches, Jim and I had bets between us. If I scored with an overhead kick, I won £10, and if Jim scored from a free-kick outside the box, I would have to pay him £10. Don't worry, though, any money that changed hands went into the charity of the day, mostly from my pocket.

One day, while we were sitting in Jimmy's house in the Croft with his wife Lana and two daughters, chatting over a cup of tea, Emma and Jodie asked me if I needed a labourer to help me, obviously thinking of Jimmy. So I said I would give it a thought. Although I had plenty of work on, the problem was, like Bobby Stokes, Jimmy couldn't drive, so it would mean picking him up from his new home, which was the annex of the house which Peter Shilton owned in the upmarket area of Southampton. It was not for me to say what had happened between Jim and his family.

Anyway, after thinking about the pros and cons, I decided to take Jim on. Our first job together was to fit a new kitchen for a policeman friend of mine. I showed Jim how to join the units together using the cordless drill. OK said Jim, and after attempting to stabilise two units, he drilled through one of his fingers. I ran to the bathroom, grabbed a white towel and wrapped it around his finger. In no time the towel was red and Jimmy was white. At that time he was not, as his book was called, *Hard Case*. He was off work for the rest of the week. When Jim came back our work seemed to carry on fine and for a few weeks all was well, apart from people reminding me that things happen in threes.

Jim was really getting to know the tools and fittings and when we had an awkward job, he was a big help to me, until we had to take a boiler from a loft area and re-site it in the kitchen. I realised that when I had disconnected the pipework, getting the boiler from the loft area down on to the landing, using the loft ladder, was not going to be easy. Anyway, I had brought some yacht rope to lower the boiler through the hatch using the loft joists. As I was nearing the opening I realised the rope wasn't going to be long enough, so I asked Jim to take the weight. Yes, he said, but I didn't realise he was still halfway up the loft ladder. The rope then slipped and Jim took the weight of the boiler. He couldn't hold it and, consequently, slipped down the ladder with the boiler following. Both knees and both trouser legs ripped and Jim lay there with the boiler on top of him, bleeding. I climbed down, lifted the boiler off him, and his first words to me were, 'I'm playing in Matt Le Tissier's testimonial tonight.'

I looked at him while cleaning up as best I could saying, 'I don't think so mate.'

Jim knew I was right, so we watched the game instead. Sorry Jim!

Going on from there, we both wondered if there was going to be third incident. Quite a few jobs came and went without any problems. Then I was asked to sort out a gas supply for a friend in Petersfield. She was going on holiday for a week, so we agreed I would sort it out while she was away. On the day we started I realised I hadn't located the area where the problem was, or where the meter was, so she said she would leave a note. Looking for the note, both of us checked normal places: garage and internally. Then

I remembered she had told me that the problem smell was coming up from the kitchen floor. So while Jim was still looking for the note, I found an area of tiles with a handle set in. I lifted the handle and exposed a trap door under the kitchen floor housing the pipework and gas meter. Just as I found the trap door, Jim found the note, but I didn't know as I was under the floor with the trap door open. As he was walking into the kitchen Jim was explaining to me what the note said, and the next thing, he was lying at my feet: both of us under the kitchen floor. I was laughing, but Jim was not, at first. Then we made a cup of tea, sat down looking at each other and laughed out loud, with me saying, 'Jim, things come in threes, mate.' 'I hope so,' was his reply.

While Jimmy was all over the place being a footballer and a celebrity, his girls meant a lot to him, and when you were around the kitchen table, over a cup of tea it was obvious all three of them felt the same about him. We still keep in touch on a regular basis. Take care mate, and you girls, including Lana.

Bobby Stokes

He scored the winning goal against Manchester United in the 1976 FA Cup Final. He was a quiet lad from Paulsgrove, who now lives with his wife Jan in Portsmouth. We became friends through football. I turned out for Portsmouth ex-professionals in charity games, while Bob and Jan worked behind the bar, running pubs.

During the working day I was out fitting central heating in houses, installing bathrooms, or fixing leaks, and thoroughly enjoying my work. Then on Sundays I was playing football for either Pompey or Southampton, picking Bob up, then after the match taking him home after a few pints with the lads.

I actually put central heating in Bob's mam and dad's house in Paulsgrove, with Bob helping me as my plumber's mate. At the end of the year Bob and Jan always invited Ann and me down to to see the New Year in with them.

Now Jan's family were entertainers. Her brother was a professional dancer working with Wayne Sleep in London. Jan and her sister ran their own dancing school, while her mam and dad were entertainers. We sometimes talk about our fantastic New Years' Eves with the family.

Jan asked me if I could call in to talk to about Bob. After our chat we agreed that I would take Bob with me as my plumber's mate, at the time paying him £6 per hour and making sure we went to a café for our lunch. We also made sure we carried a football in the van, so if we found a patch of grass and maybe a goal, we would have bets on who could do what first with the ball. That was when you saw the real Bobby Stokes. I always came second.

One of Bobby's team mates had moved up north, back to his roots, but had mixed with the wrong people regarding betting and found himself in hospital, in a bad way. So Bob and I decided to go up and visit him. The journey, some 350 miles, took us seven hours with a couple of stops. When we arrived at my sister's, she went into the kitchen to make us some lunch, while I took our gear from the car to the bedroom we were using. After ten to 15 minutes my sister came into the lounge saying, 'Food's ready', but we couldn't find Bob anywhere in the house.

My sister put the food in the oven, while our John and I went to look for Bobby. Being a miners' town, we had some thirteen pubs and three clubs. After visiting every pub and club, there was no Bobby. I then said to our John that the only club left to check was in the village where I was born, the Oakenshaw Miners' Club, only three miles away. When we arrived we walked into the bar to see about a dozen chairs circling one chair in the middle. That was Bobby's chair. The barman recognised our John and me, only to say, 'Hi boys, look who's here: "The" Bobby Stokes.'

A couple of my old mates had recognised Bob, stopped him and said, 'Stokesy, do you fancy a pint?'

And there they were, Bob and his new mates, each with a pint, listening to Bobby's version of the 1976 goal and match against Man Utd. We stayed for ten minutes, then took Bob back to my sister's, who, had it been me who had gone missing, would have thrown my dinner in the bin, but Bob sat down and ate his meal as if nothing had happened. For years Bobby Stokes' visit to the club was talked about regularly. Bobby couldn't believe he was recognised up north!

The following day we made our way to Ashington hospital to see his old team mate. They only allowed us in to see him because we had driven from Portsmouth. What a sight! He wasn't fully awake, but with two broken legs and head injuries, we felt he was lucky to be alive. After no more than 20 minutes we were asked to leave, and they gave me his ward and hospital number so we could check on his progress. He did make a complete recovery some four months later. However, Bobby came back with me, discussing our visit up north to see him, referring to how bad he looked, not knowing if mentally he would be OK.

In the end, Stokesy moved to his mam and dad's house in Paulsgrove. Then one Saturday morning my phone rang. It was Janet, with the bad news that my mate Bobby had passed away. She also asked me if I would accompany her to the funeral directors at the Co-operative in Portsmouth when Bobby was prepared in his coffin. As Jan and I walked in we were shown into the room where he was. We held each other's hand, walked up to the coffin, looked at Bobby lying there, then looked at each other and smiled, tears in our eyes. It was a release for Janet, and a loss of a close friend for me. Bobby Stokes wasn't just remembered for the goal he scored in the FA Cup Final at Wembley. To those who knew him he didn't have a bad bone in his body. They didn't have any children, but by the way they took to my young son Scott, well what might have been?

Loved you, Stokesy, and Janet.

Tony Cox, Army FA

Now, when you write a book, there are sections when you decide that you should mention friends. Well, Tony Cox for me is a definite, both in the Army, in football, and as a family friend. Tony and Maureen had two sons, who also joined the Army, however, whenever we visited them, both at Aldershot in their married quarters, and South Cerney, we saw very little of the boys.

What was Tony like as a mate, and as a footballer? Very good at both. When stationed at Aldershot he made the Corps team and the Army squad, but I always felt that 'Coxie', to his friends, should have been a boxer. Tony, Terry and I gelled as mates. All from the north east and very proud of it, we were a long way from home at Aldershot.

177

When a discussion got a bit out of hand, Terry and I would try and add a bit of humour to the conversation, but Tony would want to start an argument, which he hoped would then become a nose-to-nose confrontation and, hopefully, turn into a fight. Yet this was a friend, who was a very good soldier, and eventually became a Regimental Sergeant Major. If there was a war then you wanted Coxie on your side; then after the war was won, you found out that Coxie had started it!

However, a few years ago Tony passed away, leaving Maureen and the boys without a husband and a father, and me and my family missing a true friend. I drove up to Sheffield's Grenoside Crematorium to pay my respects and say goodbye to a true friend and colleague.

Tony, your wife and sons and friends will always love and miss you. Take care mate, and don't forget there are lots of famous boxers up there!

Roy Smith, Supporter

While I was the manager at Blackfield and Langley, I met lots of people who came to watch us and cheer us on. One of them was Roy Smith, a local lad who wouldn't miss a home game no matter what, and who would turn up at some away games when he could.

Roy would be the nicest man in the ground when we had won the game, but a draw or a game lost wasn't what he had come to watch, and he would voice his opinion face-to-face with me, if we had not taken points from a home game. I loved his attitude regarding the match he was watching: shouting his team on, and telling individuals what they should have done when they had the ball, but didn't. In his own way Roy was an entertainer for the 90 minutes plus. And we all thought that if we gave him a mike he would entertain the crowd for the whole game. I shudder to think what Roy would say when speaking to the players after a game. Yet given his attitude, I don't think there was anyone among the Blackfield and Langley supporters who didn't love him for his presence and involvement when it came to football. However, I ask you, why do people like Roy leave us earlier than they should?

Roy left us in December 2015, and yes, it was a shock when we heard the news. Once again the All Saints church at Fawley was full of supporters to say goodbye to Roy, who had entertained us all at his club.

Thank you, Roy. Just don't forget to express your football knowledge to your team in the heavenly league up there. They will love it as we have at Blackfield and Langley. Miss you loads Roy!

Davey Wilson, Royal Navy

As a young lad Davey played for his local boys' club at Pennyburn, and then moved to Kilwinning Rangers. Doing well for them, he was invited to join Kilmarnock FC. Davey didn't believe he would make it as a professional. While working under Manager Jim Fleeting, he still did not believe it so he decided to join the Navy. At the time I only knew of Davey through friends talking about him, so I went to see for myself. After the game I asked him to sign for me at Worthing. Knowing he would enjoy playing alongside Steve Riley, his Navy captain, someone I had signed prior to Davey joining us.

While we had been very successful at Worthing, the travelling due to two promotions was becoming awkward, so I decided to leave Worthing and took over as manager of Bashley, taking some of the players with me. Davey and Steve Riley had become good friends, with Davey calling my wife Ann and me 'mam and dad'. Without asking any questions, we just accepted it. After a season at Bashley Davey was asked to join Newport on the Isle of Wight, yet we still kept in touch, with Davey coming to see us whenever he could.

Davey's last season as a player down south was when he played for Bashley in the Senior Football Cup Final against Aldershot. He had played in some very good non-League clubs, having a very successful career wherever he played, not forgetting the three non-League clubs Troon FC, Saltcoats Vic F. and Auchinleck Talbot, before deciding to stop playing. During his break from playing, we saw a lot of Davey, really enjoying his visits. He also travelled to Scotland to visit friends and family, yet still called to see my family up north, which was something Davey always wanted to do.

In 2008 Davey's career took him to Gibraltar to serve as a naval Welfare Officer. He also played in matches organised by the Navy as well as offering help with their fitness and wellbeing. Later from

2013 Davey served as assistant manager to Allen Bula and held his position when the Gibraltar FA were admitted to UEFA in May 2013.

In 2016 Gibraltar made their first appearance in an official UEFA tournament, with Scotland in their group.

When Bula was dismissed as the Head Coach of Gibraltar's national team, Davey was named as head coach prior to UEFA's qualifying fixture against his native Scotland. Davey had just passed his UEFA B coaching badges. Telling you all Davey's football career has been my pleasure, especially after being his friend and manager through his well-earned career. Davey now lives in Gibraltar with his lovely wife Jo and his three fine children, and if anyone deserves how things turned out for Davey Wilson, he does. I do hope he still calls us 'mam and dad', even for fun. Ann and I are very proud of his achievements in life so far.

Micky Seymour

Micky was a midfield player when I played up front for Waterlooville. I am sure his name would be the first on the team sheet. Micky was a terrific midfield general. When I got to know him, both through work and football, everything had to be right; there was no going back for a second attempt. We played together and we worked together. He told me he had been at Southampton as a youngster, but he was released at the age of 16. Well, I think they got it wrong. Micky was an excellent player, and losing was not in his thoughts. Today he has his own flat-roofing business, and things have to be right. It was a pleasure having Micky and Phil Game in midfield at the 'Ville'. Game was another player who always played to win.

Albert McCann

Albert was another top footballer whose ability was spotted by Portsmouth at Luton Town, where he had served for a couple of seasons. He also made a few starts for Coventry City.

Portsmouth became his home with the family. He served there for twelve years, scoring goals from the wing, which he found to be his best position, while also playing in midfield and sometimes up front. But Albert didn't worry which position his manager said he was playing, as long as he was in the team.

For a small guy Albert could look after himself against the bigger defenders he was up against. His ability and pace soon made them realise they were in for a torrid 90 minutes unless they were substituted.

I got to know Albert when he stepped down from professional football and joined Waterlooville, still giving defenders headaches with his ability and experience. When he found I was a plumber he invited me to make some alterations at his home, and with us both playing for the non-League side, Waterlooville, we became very good friends. However, Albert decided to give up playing, and I had moved to Scotland to play. In April 2011 Albert was entered into the Portsmouth Hall of Fame, a well-deserved accolade. As an unassuming person he was never at the front of a conversation, whatever the lads were discussing, unless it was football, the game he loved and knew.

I enjoyed his company, but found our playing days and conversations were getting fewer. Then in early January 2014 I received a call telling me that Albert had passed away. At his service at St Joseph's Catholic Church in Havant on Thursday, 23rd January all of the footballers and friends turned out to say goodbye to a true friend.

Sleep well Albert, while giving defenders nightmares.

Cliff Huxford

Cliff was a manager I met while I was serving in the Army. He was managing Basingstoke when he invited me to the Camrose ground to discuss signing for him. I met him on a training night, which I joined in, as did Cliff, who marked me on a small side game. As I went for the ball I caught him down the shin so I stopped to check he was OK, and he told me to get on with playing the game, even though there was blood under his sock.

Little did I know at the time that Cliff was a player-manager. While I played for the club, the players around me, up top, were very good: Jenner Brown, Tony Foster, Keith Smart and Alan Tyler had all played at a higher level, and much enjoyed playing alongside these players. With Cliff playing in the side behind us, we all knew that 100% for 90 minutes plus was expected.

It was such a shame that I suffered a broken arm while playing for them, and that the Army did not allow me to sign a contract for Basingstoke. Cliff was disappointed as he wanted his first team squad on contracts. Even though I wasn't allowed to sign, Cliff allowed me to play once I was fit and ready, and as I said earlier, it was a pleasure to play for him and Basingstoke. I became good friends with my team mates and Cliff, and when I learned about his time in football it didn't surprise me that he had played at Chelsea and captained Southampton, and obviously stayed in football to be a player-manager.

I do believe anyone who got to know Cliff Huxford, whether in football or just life in general, would become in time a friend, and a true friend. I have written this, my feelings, about a man who was loved by those who knew him both in football and all walks of life. Never forgotten!

I say this in the past tense, as I had a phone call recently telling me that our friend has passed away.

Rest in peace, Cliff, and thank you for being a friend to me and all those who got to know you. I will be there to say goodbye, mate and I won't forget you. Robbo and Ann.

Peter Osgood, "The" Peter Osgood

If you wanted to locate Peter, you went to his house in Waltham Chase. If you absolutely wanted to bump into Peter, The Black Dog was a good place. But there was so much more to 'Ossie'. This was the man who made my dream a reality. He was the king of Stamford Bridge for years until he presented the accolade to Gianfranco Zola one afternoon at the Bridge, full of praise for the great Italian.

I felt so lucky being a friend to Peter, a generous man. I remember when just chatting, I told Peter that Jimmy and I were hosting a charity event for children. Peter said, 'Call round to my house and I will find something for you.'

Jimmy had brought one of his European shirts from his Liverpool days. Ann and I called round to Peter and Lynn's at Peter's invitation. Ann and Lynn chatted while Peter went to his office, looked around at the photos and trophies, and then took off the wall an original hand painting of him scoring a diving header in the FA Cup for Chelsea. At first I said no, but Peter was adamant I take the painting to the charity auction. That was Peter and it sold for £900. Brilliant!

I remember our trip to France on the coach with the Southampton ex-professionals. We stopped at the services at Liphook, as the boys wanted to buy coca cola to go with the vodka and gin which Jim Steele had brought from his pub. There was a bottle for each player, which Jim handed out when he came back from the shop, with two large coke bottles as mixers. Then off we set to Dover to catch the ferry. I must admit when we drove off the ferry into France we all seemed to be more of a football squad than earlier, with some exaggerated stories coming from each player. It was the best coach journey ever, and we entered France with the attitude that we were going to win, whatever, with Peter, our Manager and the players under the influence of vodka and Jim (sorry, gin)!

Arriving in France with our driver being the only person who knew where the competition was being held, we left the coach and took rooms in a hotel. The venue was some three miles away, but at the time not one of us would have managed five minutes of football. The competition was due to start at 3 pm that afternoon, so it was sleep that was on everyone's mind, so we got our heads down.

After a couple of hours, we got ourselves sorted, checked we were all present, and took the bus to the venue. On arrival we were all impressed. The pitch looked good, and among the side show tents there were beer tents, tents selling sportswear, soft drinks tents for the younger supporters, and to cap it all, lots of supporters, as they had ex-pros from top French, Dutch and German clubs, plus us from Southampton. Peter checked us in at the official tent only to find we were due to play our first round game at 4 pm kick-off, so he chose our starting line-up. To our surprise it was seven-a-side, with 15 minutes each way. We noticed that the pitch had been made to suit seven-a-side teams. Out we went after changing, marching on to the pitch to the tune of a brass band, with the Union Jack and Dutch flag for our opposition. Big time!

The ruling of the competition was that all players had to be over 38 years old, which we were, so on with our first-round game, which thankfully we won, given our journey and two hours' sleep prior to turning up.

After our first-round victory, I knew where the boys would be, so I made my way to the beer tent, still in my Southampton strip. There they were, with Peter asking where I had been. 'Just having a walk around in the entertainment areas,' I replied.

'Go and get changed,' Peter said, 'and relax with us.' So off to the changing rooms I went. On looking through the away changing room, which was where we'd been, I couldn't find my clothes anywhere: our changing room was empty. Now if you have been in football and travelled to venues here, there and everywhere, you know your team mates get up to pranks. So back to the beer tent I went, still in my kit, and noticed that across the board no one knew where my clothes had gone, or did they? I also went to the officials' tent, but no one had handed any clothes in.

Well, as I wandered back to the boys, still in kit, the smiles got bigger on all of the faces, letting me know something was up. After sitting with the boys for about ten minutes I glanced at this old boy, tramp, walking towards us dressed in my suit, shirt and shoes! The laughter from the boys, as I noticed, was hilarious. Up I got and got hold of the old boy, who was French, by the way, telling him, 'That is my clobber, mate.'

'No,' he shook his head, holding up his outspread hand, telling me that he paid five francs for it on a clothing stall. 'Five francs!' I said. The suit had cost me £200, handmade.

'No, no,' he kept shaking his head, while now everyone in the beer tent couldn't stop laughing: French, Dutch, German and the boys, especially Ossie. I took the old boy into the dressing room, took my playing strip off, while he reluctantly took my clothes off. We swapped, and although my clothes stank of body odour, I walked out of the dressing room to the beer tent, dressed, but smelling, with my football boots in my hand. The old boy swaggered out behind me, and no one in the area could stop laughing. It was all a great prank, set up by Peter himself, but as the old boy strutted away and the laughter died down, Peter said, 'Robbo, that's our strip, we need it.' 'Well, go and get it,' I said. The last laugh syndrome!

The tournament went well for us over the next three days, and we found ourselves in the final, against Bayern Munich. The day before the final we were queuing in the hotel for breakfast, and in front of us were three of the Bayern team talking about the forthcoming final. While serving in Germany for two and a half years I had obviously picked up the language. I heard them say that two of their players were not over 38 years old, while looking at us and laughing. As they were laughing I said, in German, 'Ah, so you have two players under-age?' and left it like that. I explained to Peter what I had overheard and he said, 'Leave it to me.' As we walked out for the final the Manager of the Bayern team looked at Ossie, saying 'Good luck,' which allowed Peter to tell him that he had two players who were under 38 years old who were involved in the final. Before he stuttered out a reply, Peter carried on saying, 'We won the war against you Germans, but didn't cheat, and we will beat you today.'

You could feel the anger in Ossie's voice, which I'm sure made us more determined to beat them. However, the referee played a big part in the outcome of the final. No, we didn't win the competition, but what a journey. And how lucky was I?

As I have said earlier Peter Osgood was a true gentleman, a great footballer and a good friend, and if they are playing football up there in the sky, Peter Osgood will be involved in some way. Everyone who knew him turned out to say goodbye on 14th March 2006 at St John the Baptist Church, Church Road, Shedfield in Hampshire.

When you played, thousands came to see you, and today they were all there to say 'goodbye. Thank you, Peter!

Ashley Vickers
Ashley Vickers is going in the 'Friends' pages in my book. Now when Ashley reads this, or someone tells him he is listed as a friend in the book, yes, he is, and my reason is out of respect. We don't go out together for a drink, or to a match, but when we do bump into each other we always discuss the game we are watching. The last time we were given the chance to chat was a while ago, when we

saw each other at Andover New Streets ground. I was managing Andover Town and noticed Ash was making his way to the dugout, to say hello. After we had shaken hands, Ash made his way back to watch the game. We bumped into each other at a golf charity day in Romsey, when a nod and a wave was our hello.

Ashley had been there and done it, not in golf but in football, winning the league by ten points at Blackfield and Langley, but was not promoted due to ground failure. He took the club to the fourth round of the FA Cup, qualifying that is, and to the last 32 of the FA Vase. Ashley wouldn't tell you that, even if you asked him, but out of respect he would tell you how well you had done with your club. That's typical of Ashley.

Alan 'Oggy' Ogden, Davie Blanch and George Lockhart

Three very good Army friends, and three very good footballers. I will start by telling you that when he left the Army, Alan 'Oggy' Ogden took a job as a prison officer, and during work experience he had qualified as an FA Coach. 'Oggy' holds a record, playing 114 competitive games in one season, which no-one yet has passed. 'Oggy' played in midfield mostly, but when a shirt needed a player, he would fill it no matter what position apart from goalkeeper. He also began his prison service job by starting a national prison workers' football friendlies competition, which to this day is still a friendlies competition between prison staff. Well done Alan!

Davie Blanch was held in esteem, both as a man and a footballer. He was another Army representative on the left side, who the opposition had to foul in order to stop. Davie was a humble friend born in Wales, and when playing was the perfect player for finding a centre forward among the opponents with the ball. Also, for a free kick he would find an area which the goalkeeper had not covered.

In the three teams I played with Davie in the Army, the Regiment, the Corps and the Army XI, he was outstanding. Well done Taffy!

George Lockhart, midfield's No 10, had talent in both feet and a football brain, which we all envied. It seems funny talking about an Irishman having a brain (yes, I am joking!), but with the ball at his feet, George was magic, and if there wasn't a pass on, he would invite his marker to the ball, creating an area for a pass, and like Blanchie (Davie), he could find the top corner when shooting. Three very good team mates to have in your side.

However, it is sad to have to tell you that when George, Micky Mister and I attended our goalkeeper, Chad Gibbons' funeral in South Wales some years ago, on his way back to Ireland George was taken ill and died. What a terrible loss!

Rest in peace George, and thank you for the memories, mate.

Dave Lewis

Dave and I go back a long time, from when we first became friends, and yes, it was football that did the trick. We bumped into each other now and then, and always found time to catch up, Dave as the home team manager, and me as the away team coach. We always discussed the possibility of working together at one club.

Dave did a very good job wherever he worked in football, from Vosper Thornycroft, then on to Folland FC, then Brockenhurst, then one of my old clubs, Bashley, in all of which Dave earned respect from his players and his club. We kept in touch as friends do, hoping some day that both of us could work together for one club, but alas, it was not to be.

When I joined Worthing as coach, since Worthing were in a different league to Dave, understandably we lost touch for a while, as I spent five seasons at Worthing, while Dave was very much in demand moving to Winchester City, Newport, Isle of Wight, and Andover Town, carrying his experience and knowledge to each club. As a person you will not find a better bloke as a friend, or to work with as an assistant. However, the shame of it is we never got to work together, yet we are very good friends. Take care Dave, and thank you, football.

Jamie Bray (Brayber)

It would be wrong of me not to include the lads who work for Jamie Bray in his recruitment company in Havant. As I mentioned earlier, Jamie was my goalkeeper when I managed Andover Town FC and while being a very good keeper he was also the life and soul of a get-together, no matter where we were. His events company organises many types of events, and raises lots of money for charities, which are always well attended.

I usually call in to see Jamie and his staff when I am in the Havant area, for a chat and a cup of tea, and am always made welcome by the staff, who have said they will help me with promoting my book. So for me that offer takes a lot of pressure off when I have it published. Thank you Jamie and the boys.

Alice and Jim Watson

During my time in the Army, including football, being posted here and there and ending up making my home in Hampshire, I have hardly mentioned Ann's mam and dad, who, before they passed away, looked after Ann and our children whenever I was away from home, whether being posted abroad or going abroad to play. When they knew we were settled in Hampshire they decided to move from their home in Plumstead in south-east London to Cowplain, which was where we ended up after a few house moves.

Jim was an ex-Army warrant officer who served through the Second World War. Alice worked in London while Jim was away and while London was a main target for bombing. Things had not been easy for them being apart for years after their marriage, but then along came Ann, their daughter, who was to become my wife in later years, and without doubt, how lucky that was. Ann was an only child so it made life better for them to be near to their daughter and grandchildren. For our children, they were perfect grandparents. Ann was happy and so was I.

Both Alice and Jim watched their grandchildren grow up and played a big part in their upbringing. They were always there when needed, and as Darren, Lisa and Scott got older they would visit them after school of their own accord.

RIP Alice and Jim, and thank you for giving me Ann, and for the love you showed your grandchildren. I hope I can be as good for my grandchildren, Henry, Adam and Rose, Darren's children; Joseph and Oliver, Lisa's boys; and Ella and Ava Joyce, Scott and Lisa's girls.

My Uncles, Tommy and Frank

Anywhere local like Bishop Auckland, Crook Town or Spennymoor, I used to ride my bike to for a Saturday morning game, with my boots, etc. in my holdall on my back. But if we played at Wolsingham or Durham, then I would need a lift, which is where my Uncle Tommy came in. My dad didn't drive, plus his shifts as a miner didn't allow him even to come and watch me when we played at home. I played for my home town youth team, Willington, which had been to Wembley in the 1951 Amateur Cup Final beating the more famous club Bishop Auckland FC in front of a full house. When I moved to Scotland and joined the Army, my Uncle Tommy travelled up to see me play on one occasion.

During my playing time as a youth, my club was and still is Sunderland, even though we have just been relegated from the Championship to League One. My Uncle Tommy asked my mam and dad if he could take me to Elland Road to watch us play Leeds United. Yes, so off we went. The journey was great, and while we only drew 2-2 I loved every bit of it. Thanks, Uncle Tommy. RIP

My Uncle Frank was on my mam's side of the family, and a lot younger than Uncle Tommy. His dad, Walter, my grandfather, was the person I was to take after regarding my love for football.

My Uncle Frank worked for British Rail and was also a Sunderland fan. Whenever there was a chance for me to go, he would pick me up and we would travel by train free of charge.

Sunderland were playing at Roker Park then, and the top attendance was around 60,000. We were drawn in the FA Cup at home to Tottenham Hotspur, who at the time were a top club in the top division. That day there was an estimated crowd of over 70,000 at Roker Park. I was 14 years old, and prior to the kick-off all the youngsters, both in the Roker end and the Fulwell end, were guided on the heads of the spectators to sit on the grass behind the white lines. We drew at Roker Park. Then at White Hart Lane in the return game they beat us, although I didn't go. Spurs went on to win the FA Cup. A great, although frightening experience, but you had to be there. It took me about an hour to find my Uncle Frank, but Sunderland vs Spurs, magic!

My Wife, Ann

There is a saying in life, 'Leave the best till last.'

When you are involved as a player, coach, manager, or a spectator that is exactly what most of us do. I know when I played at Waterlooville and they played at Jubilee Road, my wife would bring the boys, my sons Darren and Scott, to most of the home games, knowing the boys both loved football and especially when their dad was playing. The distance to the ground from the club house we lived in was no more than 50 yards. Even so Ann arranged for Lisa, our daughter, to go to her friend's up the road until the boys were old enough to go on their own. Then Ann and our daughter would go to her athletics training at the Mountbatten Centre in Portsmouth.

As our children were growing up, Ann, like a lot of mums, brought them up virtually on her own. I think the only part I played was to take them, and a few of our neighbours' children, to school if I was working locally. Most times on Saturday, Tuesdays and Thursdays I went straight to whichever club I was with at the time, and when I finally got home they were usually in bed, having first been fed and watered and helped with their homework. Like a lot of fathers I just took it for granted. Ann never complained unless one or more of the children had played up.

When Scott, our youngest, joined senior school, Ann took a job in a local school working in the kitchen so she was home when the children came home. When we moved to Silvester Road and I had started coaching, nothing changed. I was working and footballing, while Ann was working both at work and when she got home, until late. I just took everything for granted as a lot of dads do. I can honestly say I played little or no part in bringing up Darren, Lisa and Scott. That was all down to Ann, and what a great job she did!

They all gave us lovely grandchildren, and she is still looking after them now, when asked. As far as I am concerned I could not have chosen a better partner, wife and friend. Our children could not have chosen a better mum, and our grandchildren could not have chosen a better nan.

Thank you, darling for everything, and that is exactly what you did as a wife, mum and nan - everything. xx